Sent

How a Middle-Class Family

Traded Success

for God's Bigger Dream

Sent

HILARY ALAN

WATERBROOK
PRESS

Sent
Published by WaterBrook Press
12265 Oracle Boulevard, Suite 200
Colorado Springs, Colorado 80921

Italics in Scripture quotations reflect the author's added emphasis.

Details in some anecdotes and stories have been changed to protect the identities of the persons involved.

ISBN 978-0-307-73157-9
ISBN 978-0-307-73158-6 (electronic)

Published in the United States by WaterBrook Multnomah, an imprint of the Crown Publishing Group, a division of Random House Inc., New York.

WaterBrook and its deer colophon are registered trademarks of Random House Inc.

Printed in the United States of America
2013—First Edition

10 9 8 7 6 5 4 3 2 1

Special Sales
Most WaterBrook Multnomah books are available at special quantity discounts when purchased in bulk by corporations, organizations, and special-interest groups. Custom imprinting or excerpting can also be done to fit special needs. For information, please e-mail SpecialMarkets@WaterBrookMultnomah.com or call 1-800-603-7051.

"When we consecrate ourselves to God, we think we are making a great sacrifice, and doing lots for Him, when really we are only letting go some little, bitsie trinkets we have been grabbing, and when our hands are empty, He fills them with His treasures."

—BETTY STAM (February 22, 1906–December 8, 1934)

CONTENTS

FOREWORD

Jesus said discovering Him was like finding a treasure hidden in a field. If you understand the value of what you have found, what you are "giving up" doesn't seem that severe. The joy of what you've found outweighs the pain of what you lose.

In this book you'll read the story of a family—a normal, American family chasing the American dream—who discovered Jesus to be worth leaving it all behind. They had a promising career, two all-American kids with solid GPAs and bright futures, a comfortable house in the suburbs, even a couple of Volvos. And then they discovered the wonderful truth about God's love for all people and the terrible reality of how little the nations of the world know about that love.

I know the family in this story. I saw them change from being "good Christians" who participated in church. They grew into committed disciples who realized that Jesus's mission is of far more value than their own lives.

When it is all said and done, this book is about the power of the gospel. The gospel is the good news that Jesus did for us what we could not do for ourselves. He lived a life we should have lived and then died the death we were condemned to die, in our place. The gospel is God's free offer of righteousness to all who will believe.

It is impossible *really* to believe that gospel and remain the same. The Alans are normal people who took the Great Commission seriously and gained access to the power of a supernatural God. Hilary's honesty in these pages is refreshing and her candor is disarming. I was again challenged to take Jesus's sacrifice as seriously as she did.

I have had the privilege not only to pastor this family but to walk through this journey with them. I have seen God continue to use them on this side of the Atlantic as they devote their lives to discipleship, engage the nations God has brought to our doorstep, and serve in our local church. They continue to exemplify the joy, humility, and generosity of Christ.

Christian heroes are ordinary people with extraordinary faith in an extraordinary God. They do radical things in response to God's radical love for them. The Alans' story will not be your story, and what God asked of them probably will not be what He asks of you. However, these things are certain: heaven and hell are real; the Great Commission is urgent; and we all have a part to play. I pray that this book will help you discover your part in this greatest of all missions.

—J. D. Greear, author of *Gospel: Recovering the Power that Made Christianity Revolutionary*

ANSWER JUST ONE QUESTION

Everyone is living for something. Having goals in life is a good thing, and working hard to make a name for yourself and achieve something big are good things, too. That's what the American Dream is all about. Many of us spend our lives trying to have it all, or at least to be seen as someone who has it all.

We crave success. We need significance. Ultimately, we want our lives to count for something, something that matters. But in addition to all that, we would love to gain respect, power, position, and prestige, because those are things that help us feel valued.

And then there is money. Whether we admit it or not, we enjoy the things money brings. We love comfort, and we want to feel secure. These are things we build our American lives on.

But what if you were making steady progress in most of the areas of life that bring comfort, security, earthly significance, and maybe even wealth? And then you found out that you were doing life all wrong? What if that realization led you to radically change the trajectory of your life? And what if changing your life meant that you would also reroute the lives of your spouse and your teenage children?

That is what happened to my family.

My husband, Curt, and I had a life that most American couples aspire to. We had career achievements, work that fit our talents and interests, two great kids, a comfortable home in an area we loved. We considered ourselves "serious" Christians who were involved in our church and ready to serve when needs arose. It was easy to share what we had, because even after sharing we had more than enough left over. There was no earthly reason why we should start questioning the legitimacy of our lives.

But we did question it, and in seeking answers we changed just about everything that we had looked to for our security, our identity, and our place in the community.

Meaning, identity, goals, success. These things drive us, and living in America gives us ready-made ways to seek to fulfill these basic needs. What's wrong with driving a reliable car, living in a comfortable home, and sending our children to good schools where they can excel academically and shine in the areas where they have been gifted? Aren't these the standards we all reach for?

Curt and I reached for that standard and exceeded it. And having achieved the goals most of us set for ourselves, we still were asking" Who and what am I living for? Myself? My children? My career? My income? My reputation? A promotion? A bigger house? A more expensive car? Retirement?"

Maybe you have asked some of these same questions. Perhaps you have achieved far more than we had by age forty. Maybe you achieved these things long before you hit forty. It's possible you are still working hard to lay hold of your goals. Or maybe you have reached a place in life where comfort and security and status and success have lost their luster.

If you have started asking "what is it that I'm living for?", I hope reading the story of the Alan family from Chapel Hill, North Carolina, will help point you to some answers. I hope our experience will lead to a shared pursuit of how God is leading his people to fulfill the basic human needs of meaning, significance, identity, and success.

Make no mistake. I am not a woman who turned her life around as a desperate response to having suffered deep tragedy. My story is just the opposite. I was living a life that I absolutely loved. I was happy, and I had it all.

Curt and I had surpassed our dreams. I felt blessed. I certainly wasn't looking for a change. Why would I? I couldn't think of any change that would improve on the life we already had. God had a life waiting for me that I couldn't see because I was so intoxicated by my myopic definition of "a great life." I was impressed by how well Curt and I had done.

I didn't realize that I had traded life for a lie. I had no idea that my heart had grown hard and unaware of the things that matter to God. I had learned to be content with what I later came to realize was the least important aspect of life.

Here is part of the lie that is easiest for us to buy into. We are convinced that when we go into overdrive to assure the safety and comfort of our family—positioning everyone for success—that God is pleased with us. Good parents make sure their kids have everything they need to ensure a successful outcome. It stands to reason that a responsible parent does not want her children to suffer or fail. It's all about providing them with security and stability.

Here is the truth we often are blinded to: when we live for safety and comfort and success, we train our children to do the same. The most convincing lies are the ones that do the best job of mimicking what is good.

The American Dream includes providing the best home you can for your children, which in our culture is thought to be the biggest, most comfortable house you can afford. Often, living in a part of town where big house predominate makes it possible for you to help your kids form friendships among a "good" group of kids. And it makes it easier to enroll your kids in a "good" school, where they will benefit from outside activities, get into the right classes, and earn good grades—which will set them on the path to the best college. Add it all up and boom! You have the best chance of coming out with the best kid. Our family had all of these going strong, plus we had what we saw as the added bonus of having our kids in church and youth group.

It's hard to argue that any of this is something God would want to interrupt by pulling your family out of such a forward-looking way of life. Would God really want you to pursue a different kind of life?

What does it mean to change the trajectory of your life when doing so will completely change the lives of your high school and middle school-aged children? I have yet to come across a parenting book or parenting "expert" who would encourage that, especially during those sensitive years. If anything, from the moment our children are born, we work hard to build the most secure foundation possible. We want them to be well-grounded, especially in preparation for the dreaded teenage years. We lie awake at night figuring out how to combat the destructive influences that are sure to attack our children.

Most parents and even the experts would agree that the absolute worst time to uproot a child is during middle school and high school. I know parents who turned down significant job promotions during those years because they thought moving would be too traumatic, and risky, for their teenagers. Good parents don't do that to their kids, or so the conventional wisdom goes.

Not that I worried about such things. Curt and I enjoyed thriving careers in North Carolina, with no thought about moving in order to further our success. Everything was proceeding as planned for our family. Until 2002, that is. That's when God started to confront us with troubling questions about how we were living our lives. At the time it seemed to come out of nowhere. Looking back on it now, though, I can see how things were working together to get our attention.

When you are satisfied with your life and living up to the expectations that are set for good parents, it's easy not to examine your life very closely. But God got our attention and he didn't give up. So in 2006 we let go of everything that was familiar to us. Before long, Curt and I and our teenagers were living a life that was so different from what any of us had experienced before, we knew nothing would ever be the same.

It was years in the making, starting with a troubling statement made by a speaker at a conference Curt attended. From that point on, the decision to consider other options and the changes that Curt and I started making were step by step, with no indication of all that was in front of us.

We shifted from comfortable, upper-middle-class American family to American Christian emigrants to Muslim Southeast Asia. And it began with just twenty-two words: "The two greatest moments of your life are the day you are born and the day you discover why you were born."

That is what Curt heard Kirbyjon Caldwell, a megachurch pastor from Houston, say at the 2002 Willow Creek Leadership Summit. It was a "wow" moment. And when he came home and told me about it, I had the same reaction. If those words were true, then we knew something was not quite right with our carefully planned, "perfect" life.

Sure we knew the days we were born, but we didn't have a clue about the reason *why* we were born. We didn't even know that we *needed* to know why we had been born.

Finding the answer was the critical missing piece. If we could discover the reason we were born, it would make everything else make sense. So we began a quest. We became obsessed with the word *purpose*. This was around the time that *The Purpose-Driven Life* was published. "Problem solved! We'll read that book and find our purpose, which must be the reason why we were born, and all will be well!"

Or so we thought.

We took an assessment of our lives, as if that would settle things. Two college degrees, check. Solid marriage, check. A couple of great kids, check. Senior management position after years climbing the corporate ladder, check. Brand new dream home in an upscale subdivision, check. Cute dog, check. Great vacations, check. Friends, meaningful activities, involved in church, check, check, and check. As we added checks, we were starting to feel impressed with our accomplishments. Maybe we were worrying about a whole lotta nothing.

But we weren't.

God used those twenty-two words to begin to wake us up. Today, we know the reason why we were born. And knowing the reason led Curt and I on a journey that left very little of our former life intact. We left our home, our careers, our possessions, our town, friends and a church we loved, and everything that was familiar to us to move, literally, half-way around the world.

If that sounds to you like we made a huge mistake, I invite you to go on the journey with us. We moved our family to a region of the world we had thought very little about up to then. We lived in a culture we were honestly a little afraid of. And the timing of our move followed shortly behind one of the greatest natural disasters of this generation.

Did we throw away forty-plus years of accomplishments just to endanger our health, our children's safety, and our family's stability? Again, I invite you to experience what we experienced in the world's most densely populated Muslim province.

In seeing how God spoke to us during a time when we couldn't have been more satisfied with the life we already had, perhaps you will hear God reveal the reason why you were born. You might learn you are exactly where He wants you to be, or that it's time for a change. One thing is certain, there is no other question you can answer that will move you quite like this one.

Chapter 1

DECEMBER 26, 2004

Our Lives Were Changed by a Tsunami in Asia

December 26, 2004, should have been just another sunny Sunday morning on the northernmost tip of a spectacular island in Southeast Asia. Though it was the day after Christmas in the Western world, here there were no twinkling lights, turkey dinners, or piles of discarded holiday paper. It was just another day in this strict Muslim province.

Most of the locals had been awake since sunrise for the first of the five obligatory daily calls to prayer. By 9 a.m., people were moving about the city on the only non-work day of the week. Parks were filled with children, and large numbers of city dwellers had flocked to the pristine Indian Ocean beaches, a favorite gathering place for swimming, chatting, and eating freshly caught grilled fish. In the villages, women were finishing household chores. And fishermen, who never seem to have a day off, were already out to sea.

There is a phenomenon in the South Pacific known as the Ring of Fire, characterized by volcanic and geologic instability. Although earthquakes are a fact of life in this part of the world, no one was prepared for what happened that sunny morning in December. At

9:15 local time, the earth shook violently for between eight and ten minutes. The magnitude of that earthquake, the third largest ever recorded on a seismograph, registered between 9.1 and 9.3. This province of 4 million people was the closest point of land to its epicenter.

As soon as the shaking began, locals knew to take the usual precautions. They evacuated their homes to avoid being injured by falling objects or structures. But this earthquake was unlike any other. Nothing had prepared the people for what they were seeing and feeling, because they had never before experienced an earthquake of this magnitude. It wasn't enough to just get outside. The tremors were so strong the only thing people could do was to lie down in the streets. Remaining upright was impossible.

Within ten minutes, homes and buildings were flattened. Roadways and bridges were severely damaged or completely taken out. Ten minutes may not seem like a long time, if you are driving to work or preparing dinner. But it seems like an eternity when the ground underneath your feet threatens to drop away. All across the affected province, panic set in as roadways were cracked and the ground kept rising and falling like a living thing.

When the earth finally stopped shaking, there was relative quiet for fifteen minutes. The earthquake's epicenter was many miles off the coast, so it took a quarter-hour for the wall of ocean to reach shore. The first tsunami wave struck a beautiful, unspoiled coastline. But the people in the city didn't know what was happening on the coast. They were unaware that just five miles away entire villages were being annihilated. Thousands of their friends and relatives were losing their lives, and the landscape and lives in this province were changing forever.

After the first tsunami wave struck, it was followed by a second, and then a third. The waves were so deadly that hundreds of thousands of lives were claimed in a matter of minutes. The waves were high enough to knock off the top of a ten-story-high lighthouse. The same waves carried boats that were miles out at sea onto previously dry land. Wave-borne boats crushed homes and people in their paths. A huge, ten-megawatt diesel power plant that had been mounted on a barge several miles offshore landed atop several homes in the middle of a village five kilometers inland. It remains there today.

There were people living miles inland who, though unaware of the devastation being wrought along the coast, somehow knew to run. Maybe it was instinct, maybe it was panic, and maybe it was divine intervention. Many of them started running even before the deadly invading waters were visible. And those who remained behind, traumatized from the earthquake, soon saw the water racing toward them miles inland from the coast.

The dangers were mounting, and those who had not followed their instincts to run were now forced to confront what at first appeared to be minor flooding. But within seconds, low-lying areas filled with water and it kept coming. The water level rose several stories high. People were killed by advancing waters because they had no time to react.

At the time, this province had no tsunami warning or sophisticated communication system to alert the people to what was happening at the coast. In a panic, people responded the only way they knew to, they ran for their lives. Men, women, children, old and young, climbed on anything that was above what they anticipated to be flood level. But even those who tried to run were overcome by the explosion of rushing water. In seconds, deadly debris came racing into the city, as corpses, body parts, vehicles, fragments of buildings, boats, and the debris of unidentifiable wreckage was swirling in blackened, poisonous waters. The screams of fleeing city dwellers were suddenly silenced as the waters took over.

In a matter of minutes, approximately 230,000 human lives were claimed by the earthquake and subsequent tsunami. And while this cataclysmic, life-changing event took place in Southeast Asia, I was half a world away and completely unaware.

∞

When the December 26, 2004, tsunami hit Southeast Asia, it was still Christmas night in North Carolina. I was safe in my comfortable home, doing what I'd been training all of my life to do. I was living for myself.

At the time of the greatest natural disaster of my generation, I was a forty-one year old, upper-middle-class, Christian American living a charmed life. The only thing I really cared about was making life as wonderful as possible for the four of us. So while thousands of people were losing their lives on the opposite side of the world, I was packing for a winter vacation in Florida.

The next day, news outlets in the West were beginning to report the horrific events that had transpired in the East. I was traveling south with my family in our Volvo station wagon. Thankful for the car's heated seats and munching on snacks from Whole Foods, my thoughts involved the hope that we would make good time as we headed south toward Crystal River, Florida. The four of us were looking forward to swimming with manatees.

In the late morning we took a break at a rest stop just across the state line in South Carolina. It felt good to stretch our legs after driving the first few hours of a ten-hour road trip. It was a beautiful, sunny day in the southeastern United States and the temperatures were mild for late December. But when I got back in the car, tragedy struck.

My seat belt wouldn't latch.

I tugged and pulled and then yanked on the belt, but it wouldn't click. I wasn't going to ride on I-95 in the front seat of a car without a seatbelt, but I didn't want to spend the rest of my vacation riding in the less-comfortable back seat either! There wasn't anything we could do to fix a seatbelt at a rest stop in South Carolina, so I climbed into the back seat between my son, Jordan, and my daughter, Molly. Curt got back on the highway and I started calling Volvo roadside assistance, demanding immediate attention. This was definitely a case where quick action was *really* needed.

We found a Volvo dealer in Savannah, Georgia. The service attendants were polite, even though they were stuck having to work on the day after Christmas. For my part, I was thankful they were working so they could rescue us when we really needed it.

We were led to a comfortable waiting room where a television was tuned to a news channel. As we pulled lunches out of our cooler, we noticed the TV was showing footage of a disaster on the other side of the world. Since I was the one distributing sandwiches and drinks, I was only half watching and half listening. I was more concerned with getting everyone fed so we could be on our way as soon as the seatbelt was repaired. While I ate my lunch and waited for what I considered to be my own little road-trip tragedy, I saw the first images of the Asian tsunami. CNN was covering the disaster, broadcasting from Phuket, Thailand.

"Wow. That looks really bad."

I felt for the people who were suffering as the result of the earthquake and tsunami, but with typical feelings of detachment. None of this was happening within the borders of the United States.

I'll be honest. The distance I felt from what I was seeing was both emotional and physical. I was much more concerned with how much time we would lose due to the interruption of the broken seat belt.

Plus, I had never heard of Phuket, Thailand. To my way of thinking, if a natural disaster wasn't affecting the United States, let alone the interstate highway between North Carolina and Florida, I didn't think it was anything we needed to be overly concerned about.

Just as we finished our lunch, a service technician appeared and said the magic words: "OK, you're all set!"

It turned out that this stop had not been too inconvenient. And it was so much nicer to eat in a comfortable waiting room rather than a roadside rest stop.

"Wonderful! Let's get to Florida!!"

The events we had seen on CNN were quickly forgotten. We were more focused on the quick service we'd received at the Volvo dealership. We drove to Florida and had a wonderful vacation, just as we had planned. And I was not forced to ride in the uncomfortable back seat, squeezed in between my kids.

∞

In 2004, my family and I were intoxicated by the American Dream. Curt was an IT director at SAS Institute, the largest privately owned software company in the world. (SAS was hailed in 2010 and again in 2011 by Fortune magazine as the Best Company to Work For in America.) He had a plush corner office, a reserved parking space, a six-figure salary, a thirty-five hour work week, four weeks of vacation every year (with an extra week at Christmas), and a nationally recognized benefits package. He often travelled to Germany, the company's European headquarters, earning enough frequent flyer miles to take us on vacations to Maui, London, and Paris.

We lived in a brand-new house in an upscale subdivision. We both drove new cars and we had two beautiful, healthy kids. We thought we were serious Christians because we attended a Bible-teaching church every week where we were "involved." We considered God to be a priority in our lives. No question, we had it all.

The truth is we were living for nothing more than the advance-

ment of our own little kingdom. With every raise my husband received, we increased our standard of living. Though my husband's job
provided well for our family and enabled me to stay at home, I took on
a part-time position as a teacher's assistant at our daughter's elementary
school. I enjoyed the work, and I enjoyed having "just a little extra
money" for ourselves. (The truth is, no matter what our salaries were
we always wanted more.) We were convinced that an extra $10,000 or
so would make the difference and get us everything we wanted. But
we'd bring in $10,000 more and find it never quite did the job. We
could never be fully satisfied with what we had.

When I went shopping, for groceries or clothes, I bought what I
wanted, not considering what was on sale or clipping coupons. That
was too much trouble. I didn't shop in expensive stores or pricey bou-
tiques, because I considered myself low maintenance and did most of
my shopping at the Gap, Old Navy, and Target. Since I bought clothes
off clearance racks, I considered myself fairly frugal. We put all of our
regular expenses on an airline affiliated credit card, which we paid in
full every month in order to earn frequent flyer miles. That way we
could count on taking even better vacations in the future. Since we
were not carrying any debt, and we were earning free airfare for future
vacations, we considered ourselves to be financially wise.

Our approach to life extended to the way we practiced our faith.
We attended church, had our kids participating in church activities,
and Curt and I were also involved. We lived across the street from our
pastor, and considered him and his wife to be good friends. We prayed
and we read our Bibles. But when it came to the Bible, we preferred to
read selected passages that we found inspiring or consoling. We weren't
reading the Bible with an openness to being changed by the truth we
found there.

And then, as we drove to Florida on our December vacation, we became aware of a devastated region in Southeast Asia. We didn't realize it, of course, but God was planning to use the widespread destruction and loss of life to reverse the trajectory of our lives. Within weeks of our stopping in Savannah to get a seatbelt fixed, God would interrupt the lives of two adults in their forties, a fourteen-year-old boy, and a ten-year-old girl. He had future plans for us that involved resigning from our jobs and selling our home, our cars, and our possessions. He wanted us to take a completely different path in life.

"Then Jesus told his disciples, [']If anyone would come after me, let him deny himself and take up his cross and follow me. For whoever would save his life will lose it, but whoever loses his life for my sake will find it. For what will it profit a man if he gains the whole world and forfeits his soul[']?" (Matthew 16:24).

If you are single and have read advice about being intentional in dating, you are familiar with the advice regarding a DTR, a conversation designed to Define the Relationship. It's important that you not assume that the man or woman you are interested in shares the same level of attraction to you. In our case, the Asian tsunami forced our family to examine our relationship with God. It was time for a DTR with Him.

We loved God, but were we ready to serve Him and other people without holding anything back? Were we prepared to obey Him even when it would lead us to do things with our lives that we never dreamed of, or even knew were possible?

God called us to give up everything so we could trust in Him alone. He called us during a time when the nation's economy was weakening and the rate of unemployment promised to rise. Curt and I both had job security and high combined salaries, but God called us to give that up so we could earn less than what we had made when we were first married in 1985. He called us to homeschool a rising middle-schooler and a high-schooler, who had been in traditional schools all their lives. He asked us to leave a comfortable life that we had worked hard to create. He wanted us to go somewhere we previously weren't even aware existed.

God was not interested in how good we were at serving ourselves. He took us to the other side of the world to serve Him, and to live among a people group we had never before heard of, and frankly were a little afraid of. Curt was an IT specialist, I had worked in public relations and education. Neither of us were experienced in disaster relief or community development. We were not veterans of short-term missions trips. But the Alans are living proof that God doesn't call the equipped, he equips the called.

There was nothing in our background to indicate that we would succeed in helping Muslims who didn't speak English and who were suspicious of Westerners. We had no experience or qualifications that gave us expertise in helping people rebuild their lives after a devastating tsunami.

There was only one reason why God would choose the four of us. We learned that God delights in using ordinary people to do very extraordinary things. He delights even more in reversing the trajectory of a life, pointing us away from ourselves and toward Him. In fact, that's kind of the point.

But we didn't know that yet. This is our story.

Chapter 2

TIME FOR A CHANGE

Look for the Life That God Is Just Now Revealing

God is working in your life even when you don't realize it. He used a number of events preceding the 2004 tsunami to lead us to the point where we would start responding to his leading. Some things are better seen in hindsight. I believe that if we recognized all the things God was doing at the time He was doing them, we might have run in the opposite direction.

"No thanks, we're good. We kind of like our nice, comfortable life!"

In 2003, Curt, the kids, and I were attending a nondenominational church in Chapel Hill. We had bought a house across the street from the church's pastor, Mark, and his wife, Libby. They were about ten years older than we were, and much wiser. Due to shared interests and a desire to walk with God through life, the four of us became close friends.

Curt had a lot of responsibility at work, leading a large staff and managing a multimillion-dollar budget. He was the first person I knew who carried a Blackberry, and he was constantly checking it, weekends included. Although I admired his work ethic and the success he had achieved, I knew he wasn't in the right line of work for who he was, deep down. Whenever I would mention that his work didn't seem to fit with who I knew him to be, his answer was always the same: "It's a means to an end."

That "end" was our comfortable lifestyle. Curt took his role as provider seriously, and while he found his role at work stimulating, and was good at what he did, I knew it wasn't *him*. It wasn't just that he was an English major in college and was now working as an IT director. And it wasn't that he was working with several "marketing types" whose temperaments were the opposite of Curt's ordered, conscientious demeanor. I just knew that a career in the software industry, or any other big business, wasn't him.

While he is a great leader and visionary, Curt has a pastoral, servant heart that didn't seem well-suited to the high-tech industry. But his hard work had earned promotions to director. Fitting his career to who he was didn't seem to bother Curt as much as it did me. He was well paid and we were well provided for, and he had a job he was good at. Curt was respected and known for his integrity. Wasn't there great value in being a good example of integrity and an honest work ethic to our kids and to the people he worked with?

One day he came home from playing disc golf with Mark, the pastor who lived across the street. Mark had asked Curt if he would consider taking on responsibility for starting and leading community ministry, a major ministry area at the church. Community ministry helps church members get directly involved in the needs of their community and helps the church be relevant to the community in which it is located. Curt's desire to help people, his humble personality, and his leadership skills must have seemed like a great fit to Mark. That night, Curt tried to talk to me about it. I was less than supportive.

"*What?* In what free time are you supposed to do *that*? You need to spend the little free time that you do have with me and the kids. Don't they have paid staff to do that work? Why are they asking church members who already have full-time jobs to do it?"

Although Mark was a close friend, I couldn't understand how he could ask my husband to take on such a big volunteer responsibility. He knew how busy and overworked Curt was. He knew that family was important to us. I immediately dismissed the idea, too selfish and immature to consider that Mark might see something in Curt that I didn't want to acknowledge...yet.

God had begun working, and there was more in store. He was about to start working on my stubbornness and my hard, selfish heart. He used events that were stressful and, at the time, relatively unimportant. Little did I know that they would turn out to be significant turning points in our lives.

The first happened in August 2003 while we were vacationing at Sunset Beach, North Carolina, our favorite place to unwind. We had use of a friend's beach house for a week. We could drive three hours from home and be free from the Blackberry, bills, and the everyday responsibilities of life. We could rest! The beach at Sunset is wide and unspoiled. Peace and quiet is everywhere. Our beach week was something the four of us anticipated all year long.

One evening we decided to go out for dinner. We drove toward the last town in North Carolina before you hit the state line. We were headed to Dockside, our favorite restaurant that served a particular local style of seafood. We'd order huge plates of shrimp and hushpuppies and eat until we were stuffed. That night we were celebrating Curt's and Jordan's shared birthday, and it was restful to overlook the ocean as we ate dinner.

Afterward we walked to our car so we could head back to Sunset

Beach. But there was a problem. Our car refused to start. There wasn't even any sound when we turned the key.

We had no cell phone because I made Curt leave his Blackberry back home in Chapel Hill. So Curt went back into the restaurant, asked for the yellow pages and a telephone, and started calling towing companies.

Since it was a weekend evening, he assumed most of them would not answer the phone. And the ones that did answer, he fully expected would refuse to drive to our location so far from any populated area. We felt really, really stuck, and really, really alone.

Though it was a busy night and the restaurant was full, the staff sensed something was troubling the man on the phone who kept combing through the Yellow Pages. When they learned of our plight, they recommended that we seek help from a local man known as Captain Tommy, a shrimper whose boat was docked beside the restaurant.

"He fixes everything," they said.

We headed out to the dock and found Tommy, a rugged, middle-aged man who was preparing to go home after having been on the ocean since four that morning. We explained our situation and asked if he knew who or how we could get some help. He ducked inside his boat and reappeared with jumper cables.

We thought we'd be on our way in just a few minutes. Nope. Tommy pulled his truck up to our car, attached the cables, and again, the car did nothing. It was now past 8 p.m. and Tommy had been up for more than sixteen hours. He suggested that we may need a new battery. We asked if there was any place nearby where we could get one. He recommended a Wal-Mart, about forty-five minutes from the restaurant. Stuck without a car, in a town where we didn't know anyone, with no public transportation and no phone, we were desperate.

So we turned to the one thing we could always count on. Our money. We offered Tommy fifty dollars to drive us to Wal-Mart and back.

He said, "OK, but I have to go home first. I'll be back in twenty minutes."

He had a truck that was running fine, he was exhausted from work, we were simply vacationers, and he was leaving without us. *Oh great,* we thought, *that's the last we'll see of Tommy.*

It was getting dark, and I can't say we were feeling confident about Tommy. But twenty minutes later, he came back, just as he said he would. He offered his docked boat to the kids and me while we waited for him and Curt to get back from Wal-Mart. He had a TV on the boat, and our wait was looking to be at least ninety minutes before they returned. Not wanting to inconvenience him any more than we already had, especially given that he was already going out of his way to help people he didn't know, I thanked him and declined. The kids and I waited in our dead car.

We talked, sang, and told stories. It wasn't long before we started to attract attention. People noticed that the same mom was sitting in the passenger seat with two young kids in the back seat, but no one was in the driver's seat. People asked if we were all right. Some of them offered to bring us food. It was almost funny.

By the time Curt and Tommy returned, it was well past 10 p.m. Fortunately, as soon as they put the new battery in, the car started. Curt handed Tommy two twenty-dollar bills and a ten. And Tommy the shrimp boat captain, who had been up for close to twenty hours, handed the two twenties back. He only wanted ten dollars, which probably covered only the gas that was used going to and from Wal-Mart.

Curt and I were humbled that this hardworking fisherman would be so generous with his time and help, even though we were strangers to him. Honestly, we were people that otherwise would have easily overlooked him. How many times had we been to dinner at Dockside and never noticed the shrimper whose boat was docked alongside the restaurant? Though we had likely taken an after-dinner walk along that dock and probably had walked right past Tommy's boat, we didn't give thought or attention to the people around us. We were oblivious to people like Tommy because we were so consumed with ourselves.

As moved as I was by Captain Tommy's generosity, it was just a start in God's work to soften my heart. As soon as we left tiny Cala-bash, North Carolina, that evening, we went right back to living our comfortable life that centered around ourselves.

A month later, back home in Chapel Hill, we were heading to a friend's wedding in Jamestown, about an hour away. We got on the entrance ramp to I-40 headed west, and we had a typical man vs. woman disagreement about whether the car had enough gas. The fuel gauge was on E. The warning light remained unlit, but the needle told me everything I needed to know.

I said, "Honey, shouldn't we get some gas *before* we get on I-40?"

Curt gave me the typical male response: "Don't worry, we have plenty. We'll stop in Burlington."

For you out-of-staters, Burlington is thirty minutes away. I kept picturing us getting stuck in heavy traffic and running out of gas be-fore we could reach Burlington. As the needle started to fall below E, about thirty minutes after we left Chapel Hill, we pulled into a gas station. And when Curt got out of the car to pump the gas, something happened for the first (and hopefully last) time in our marriage.

He reached back to his hip pocket to get his credit card and couldn't believe what he found there. We had been married nearly twenty years, and I can't recall one time when we had gone anywhere in the car and Curt had not taken his wallet. Shaking his head, he confidently asked for my purse. And...this also had never ever happened before…I realized I had left my purse at home. I never ever forget my purse, because it contains two of my life's essentials: lip balm and a water bottle. I *always* have my purse with me because I can't go anywhere without water and lip balm. We were stuck—unable to get to the wedding, unable to get home, unable to gas up the car. And once again, we were without a phone, because I had asked my husband to put his Blackberry away on weekends.

We discussed our limited options, which really amounted to only one. We hoped that the fact that all four of us were well dressed and clearly on our way to a wedding would help persuade a stranger to believe our story. So Curt went into the gas station's mini mart and explained our situation to the young girl working at the register.

He said, "If you will lend me just five dollars to put enough gas in my car to get to our friend's wedding, I will take down your address, and I promise that I will mail you a check for ten dollars as soon as we get home."

Hey, she could double her money just by helping us out of a tight spot. The girl looked like she'd walked a hard road. Her face was scarred from burns, she had several missing teeth, and her manner of speech indicated that she came from a background very different from ours.

She responded, "I only have ten dollars until payday next week, but I'll give you five."

She had ten dollars to last her the best part of a week. And she willingly gave us *half* of all the money she had. She must have known that giving a stranger half her money was not a good risk to take. And yet she did it. Cheerfully.

∞

For the second time in a little over a month, we were in a situation where nothing we could do for ourselves would help. Our functional god, our income, had proven to be untrustworthy. We needed the help of people we otherwise would have overlooked, and who had every reason to resent us because we had so much more than they did materially. But they didn't let that keep them from offering help that we desperately needed.

The story doesn't end with the generous mini-mart employee. We arrived at the wedding only to realize that the only person we knew at the event was the bride! Again, we didn't have enough gas or money to get back home. Long story short, we made a new friend at the wedding, we made it home safely, and the girl from the mini-mart got her check.

Do you think God had gotten through to us by that time? We couldn't easily ignore the lessons He was trying to teach us through Captain Tommy and the young woman at the gas station. He was pointing out the importance of community, of taking care of people and loving the people around you. In essence, being the church wherever you are.

Mark had been right when he asked Curt to take charge of the church's community ministry. He had seen in Curt what I had long seen, that Curt is wired to help people. How long had I been telling Curt that his job was "so not him," and then when an opportunity came along to work in accordance with his giftings, who stood in his way? Me! I was convicted. And ashamed.

That fall Curt began leading community ministry at our church, understanding that this was not stealing time from his family but simply an act of obedience to God. We knew that God was leading us in a new direction.

When Curt took on the community ministry—with an emphasis on serving those around us—I saw him come alive in a way I had never seen before. I knew that for the first time in his life, he was sensing there was a plan for his life.

Curt set up our church as a regional drop-off site for Samaritan's Purse. Samaritan's Purse distributes shoeboxes full of toys at Christmas to children in areas where they otherwise would not receive anything, to demonstrate God's love in a tangible way. They also partner with churches all over the world to share the gospel in the areas where the shoeboxes are distributed. This project was something our children and I enjoyed helping Curt with, and it was exciting to see our whole church embrace it. In working on this project, Curt made several contacts in the community, some of whom would play important roles in what was to come farther down the road.

Another project Curt led was the distribution to our church members of small cardboard boxes that contained a specific grocery list. The list specified items that would fill the box; it represented enough food to feed one family of four for a week. The filled boxes were to be returned on a particular Sunday when they would be distributed to families in need in the Chapel Hill area. The whole church rallied around this project, and boxes were stacked high and deep on the Sunday that they were due back. It was exciting to see Curt lead our church in loving our community well.

For the first time in our life together, Curt was working in full accordance with the gifts God has given him. And he was changed. His natural compassion, sensitivity toward others, his humble servant heart, and the leadership skills he'd developed over eighteen years in business were perfectly suited to guide the church in this new area.

I had always thought it ironic that my husband was an IT director. That was not the man I knew him to be. Though he was definitely good at what he did, and was absolutely gifted at empowering talented people, developing and leading teams, and working well with difficult people, he wasn't a marketing type, or a computer geek, or even just a "suit." I knew there was something that just wasn't right about how he spent the majority of his time. But whenever I would talk to him about it, he would tell me that he did enjoy his work. And he would remind me that he considered it his way to provide a comfortable lifestyle for his family.

I enjoyed our life, but deep down I wondered if he was doing it all just so our children and I would have what our culture has imposed on us as *the* goal in life. I knew my husband was the kind of man who would sacrifice his own happiness if that was necessary to make me and our children happy. Although I was moved at his willingness to sacrifice for us, I loved him too much to see him spending his life that way. When he started working in community ministry, I probably told Curt every day: "This is what you should be doing. This is your heart, I can see it! This is what you were meant to do."

While he appreciated my encouragement and enthusiasm, he saw it as more of a hobby. Who in ministry could maintain the kind of life we had worked hard for and grown accustomed to? And while I appreciated what his hard work Monday through Friday provided for us, in my heart I knew he was made to serve God and others in a very different manner.

As time went on, Curt told me he thought it would be amazing to make a career out of doing what he was doing for the church. But we both knew that making such a change would dramatically alter our lifestyle. The truth is we wanted our cake and we wanted to eat it too. We hadn't considered it a matter of making a *lifestyle* change, we were only focused on a possible career change. We wanted to serve God, but we wanted to be able to hold on to our nice life too.

Chapter 3

THE CALL

When God Gets through to You

In 2004 we felt God leading us to leave the church we had been in for four years. At the time it was a hard decision, and it didn't seem to make sense. But I would later realize that it was the next step in following God's plan. We began attending The Summit Church in Durham, which at first seemed like a strange fit. It was about a forty-minute drive from our home, and at that time few people from Chapel Hill were attending there—other than students from the University of North Carolina.

Curt resigned from his role as coordinator of community ministry in the Chapel Hill church, and I encouraged him to meet with the pastors at The Summit. I thought there might be a role to fill in community ministry. He met with some of the staff, but things were, in our opinion, progressing too slowly. Had we done the wrong thing by moving to a new church? Why would God lead us here if it meant Curt had to give up the role I was sure he had been born for? We both felt frustrated, not yet understanding why God had called us here.

Curt had his own questions. He began to meet with J. D. Greear, the senior pastor of The Summit. Curt shared that he believed God could be calling him to do something other than his IT director role at SAS, but he wasn't sure how to discern a specific leading from God. I hoped their ten-year age difference, J. D. being younger, wouldn't be a barrier. I didn't want J. D. to assume that Curt was going through a mid-life crisis, and that it would soon pass. Beyond that, a mentor is usually someone who's older. I mean, what forty-two-year old man looks to a thirty-two-year old for advice? Shouldn't it be the other way around?

We knew that Curt had gifts and talents that were best used in service to the Lord, but he wasn't finding a role at The Summit. And his role at SAS was becoming less and less fulfilling. He wasn't satisfied any longer to keep working just to maintain our standard of living. Now he had caught a glimpse of a very different possibility, and he couldn't ignore it.

Thankfully, J. D. encouraged Curt to seek the Lord's will through reading the Bible more diligently, purposefully asking God to show him, in daily reading, what God was asking him to do next.

J.D. said at the time, "Just put your 'yes' on the table, Curt. 'Yes Lord, I will do what you ask me to do and go where you send me. No conditions.' And then wait for him to answer. Your job is to put and keep that 'yes' on the table, because believe me, if you do that, He is going to answer."

He was right. Despite my feeling that we weren't getting the immediate answer my restless heart wanted, God was weaving together a chain of events in response to our putting our "yes" on the table.

When we made the trip to Florida to swim with manatees, God had already been at work in our lives. He continued speaking to us through the open-handedness of strangers, and after we returned home we attended a prayer service at The Summit. It was January

2005, and J. D. had just returned from leading a volunteer short-term ministry team to Thailand. He spoke about a side trip he had made to a Southeast Asian island to learn about relief efforts that were underway following the devastating tsunami just a few weeks before. J. D. had previously worked in that part of the world teaching English.

He announced to everyone gathered that evening for prayer: "I met with the folks on the ground in Southeast Asia and they need as many of you as we can send, for as long as you can go. We need people with construction, water-purification, and medical experience to go."

I sensed this was something Curt could help with, and part of me wanted to elbow him as a way of saying, "Go!" But I didn't. Even though I had never hesitated to offer encouragement, I believe that night God kept my arm by my side. He wanted Curt to volunteer in response to Him and not me.

Curt stood up and went forward to join others who were ready to help with disaster-relief efforts. I almost gasped with thankfulness, excitement, and pride.

One of the pastors took his name and contact information, and made notes on his experience. I rightfully wondered if the pastor was confused about why a businessman with no experience in the three needed areas would volunteer. All the pastor said was "Uh, OK, we'll let you know."

Curt had followed J.D.'s advice and put his "yes" on the table. It's one thing to tell God that if anything comes along that he might want you to do, you'll be there to do it. But there is a tangible difference in actually following through. When the invitation is issued, standing up and saying, "yes, Lord" is far different from thinking about it as a distant possibility.

Curt is normally the most patient person I know. But as the days passed, he became uncharacteristically anxious to hear something back from the people at The Summit.

He called and emailed the pastor he had given his contact information to. At one point, he even emailed his resume. After all, isn't that what people do when they apply for a job?

He had scheduled some business travel in March, and while he was attending an IT meeting in Boston, he received a phone call. It was one of the pastors from The Summit.

"Curt, I got a call from the folks working on the ground in Southeast Asia. They need someone with exactly your business experience to manage all the relief funding that's coming in. They need someone who can write project proposals to channel the necessary funds to get the work started. They want to know when you can leave and how long can you stay."

I was shopping at Target when my cell phone rang. Curt was calling to let me know that he was going overseas to help with disaster relief. When he initially volunteered during the prayer service, we knew he didn't meet any of the stated qualifications. But he could, and did, offer *himself.* Through talks with the people already working in the area, the pastor who was organizing the team saw that Curt was exactly the person they needed.

Curt returned home from Boston and we discussed the timing of his trip to the tsunami-ravaged island. He would use his remaining three weeks of vacation and request an additional three weeks unpaid leave of absence from his job, to free up six weeks to serve. As we waited for this proposal to be approved at work, we felt a million different emotions, realizing that something we'd waited for and hoped for, that had felt like a remote possibility, was now *real.*

∞

Neither of us knew much about Southeast Asia, other than it must be a region close to China. We pulled out a globe and found the precise location where my husband would be sent. After we Googled the city where he would be working, we had even more questions. What about the frequent earthquakes? What if there was another tsunami while he was there? And what about the daily violence in that area? The longest-running civil war in history was still going on in the area Curt was headed to.

Aside from the threat of armed violence and the likelihood of natural disasters, there was the matter of cultural and religious differences. Curt would be living in one of the strictest Muslim areas in the world. What if, as a westerner showing up in this volatile region, Curt was targeted?

What if the wrong faction found out he was a Christian, especially an American Christian? Could he be kidnapped? Would he be harmed, or even killed?

Another concern I had was that adequate medical care and clean water were simply not available in this city. The area had been devastated by the earthquake and tsunami, and people were still trying to rebuild their lives. Infrastructure and the standard institutions of organized society were far from back to normal.

What if Curt became seriously ill and couldn't obtain adequate medical care. What if he…died? I was sending my husband and the father of my two children, for six long weeks, to a very unstable and seemingly unsafe place. What had we gotten ourselves into?

Just as Curt's decision was becoming real to me, it suddenly became scary, too. I remember the two of us lying in bed, literally counting the cost. That probably wasn't the wisest thing to do, seeing as how we needed to get to sleep! We recognized there were no guarantees of safety. But we knew God was directing all the steps to get him there, so we decided it was worth it. We were learning the meaning of discipleship. It is a matter of hearing Jesus's call and then saying yes. So even with anxiety over what might await Curt overseas, we knew that when God tells you to do something, you do it. Not going would be disobedience, something we were not willing to do.

Whatever the cost, even if it meant that he would pay the ultimate price, it was worth it, simply because we knew who had called him there. Following Jesus in obedience is worth risking our life, because He is *that* trustworthy.

It wasn't long before Curt received approval from SAS to take six weeks off from work. The damage left behind by the tsunami was still making news, and as word got around of his plans, Curt was seen at the company as a great humanitarian. Some people at the company thought it would make good publicity to send one of their own to assist in such a historic, worldwide effort. We weren't comfortable with that, choosing instead to protect the security of the workers who were already on the ground, along with Curt's personal safety in such a politically and culturally sensitive area. We made it clear that we appreciated people's interest and support, but declined offers of their direct involvement.

We prepared our hearts and began organizing the details of filling out visa paperwork and getting necessary immunizations. We also learned that one thing you do not want to do before you consider an overseas assignment is visit the U.S. Department of State travel warning website.

I tell you this so you can avoid making the mistake I made. I went to the website, which is where I learned that dengue fever, known as "break bone fever" and a sometimes-fatal condition, is a common disease in that part of the world. I checked on the city where Curt would be based and learned about the prevalence of dengue and malaria, as well as the unreliable and unsafe water supply and a variety of dangerous bacteria. The State Department made no bones about it: Americans were strongly advised not to travel to the city where my husband was headed.

Again, my fears were distracting me. And then, despite all the warnings and worries, we decided it was worth it. This was a call from God, and we had no choice but to walk forward in obedience. We knew we could count on Him to be faithful and to provide, not just for Curt on the other side of the world, but for me and the kids while we waited for him. It had to be from God, because He had repeatedly confirmed it through His Word, through Godly counsel from J. D. and others, and because this was something we never could have orchestrated on our own.

Some Christians like to say, "The safest place to be is in the center of God's will." It looks good on a plaque, but I strongly disagree with that idea. God's will is revealed to us without any guarantees or assurances of safety. Sometimes God calls people to sacrifice their lives for the sake of His Kingdom. Anyone who has died a martyr's death would surely say that being in the center of God's will was *not* the safest place to be. But in place of safety, God grants peace. The center of God's will is absolutely the most peaceful place and the most obedient place to be.

Jesus makes it clear when he said, "Follow me" (Matthew 4:19. As Curt and I considered Jesus's call, the only response was "Yes, Lord."

∞

Curt left for Southeast Asia on June 3, 2005. Our parting at the airport was a happy one. It wasn't a goodbye, it was a commissioning. Our kids and I were supportive in every sense of the word. We were so proud of Curt that I wanted to let everyone at the airport know that my husband was going to Southeast Asia to help people rebuild following the tsunami. He was definitely a hero in our eyes.

I didn't care what it would be like for the family to lose almost a month of my husband's salary. I just wanted Curt to go where God was leading him.

Once he arrived at his final destination, almost exactly half-way around the globe from North Carolina, the emails started coming in. "I can't possibly describe what I am seeing. The work being done here is nothing short of miraculous."

Curt described the situation he was entering into. "The devastation is incredible. The earthquake was massive enough to sink the entire city another 1.5 meters (almost 5 feet!) deeper into the earth. For a place that is already below sea level, it meant that the damage that the waves caused was even worse. You couldn't imagine that water could be so powerful, but it was. In one area I was in today, you could still smell the stench of death. And the sense of profound sorrow was overpowering. You look around and you wonder, 'where do you possibly begin?' It is clear that I am where I am supposed to be right now. I continue to pray that I can help, that I can provide encouragement to the people that have committed their lives to this service, and that miracles may continue to be harvested from the ashes of such a tragedy."

A few days later he sent another email, this one with a picture of himself attached. He wrote: "Worked all morning on a set of houses we're building to restore a village. Pre-tsunami, there were 4,000 villagers, and now only 50 remain, mostly men who were out fishing when it hit. We work side by side with the men. When they stop, we stop. One brought us coffee—very rich and very sweet. Hit the spot. I'm filthy, smelly, and feeling great. Amazing. So even though I am really dirty and sweaty in this picture, I thought you would enjoy seeing me *here*."

I have come to refer to that photo as the Isaiah 26:3 picture. Because as soon as I opened it, I saw this verse: "You keep him in perfect peace whose mind is stayed on you, because he trusts in you" (Isaiah 26:3.

I looked at my husband in the photo, "filthy, smelly, and feeling great." In his eyes and all over his face the peace of God was evident. That was a peace I rarely saw when Curt was immersed in his work as an IT director. Gone was the stress and the worry and the frantic pace of maintaining a comfortable life. This wasn't simply a relaxed look like I would see on vacation, after he had had a few decompression days. This was God-given peace and the first experience of his God-ordained purpose. Why else would my husband's face be radiant with joy when he was in the Third World, with no access to clean water, working in 100-plus degree temperatures, in a city where he heard gunshots at night—constant reminders of the ongoing civil war.

Add it all up—natural disaster, unfathomable loss of life, destruction that spread inland miles from the shore. Curt was working in the heart of the greatest natural disaster of our generation. And yet the peace he experienced was undeniable.

As I looked at his photo, I realized that in my comfortable American life I had only read about this type of peace. It was something I desperately wanted, but never had I learned a way to find it. I realized I didn't need to read The Purpose Driven Life, because Curt had already found it. When I looked at his photo I knew our life was about to change.

God sent me that picture of Curt. Looking back on the events of the last several years, I see that the Lord first made me aware of our need to change. That is when I wanted to nudge Curt at the prayer service. And then Curt, on his own, responded to the call for workers in Southeast Asia, showing that he had heard the call. Then I saw and heard the truth of Isaiah 26:3 in the photo of filthy, smelly, beaming

Curt. That made the call sure for all four of us.

I think God spoke to me first because I was the one who probably seemed a little reluctant. I had been encouraging Curt to use his gifts in ministry, but at the same time I was holding back. I didn't want new adventures with God to disturb our life too much. I'd been holding Curt back because I loved the comfortable lifestyle he provided for us. God had to break me of that attachment before Curt could respond to God's call.

Curt must have wondered if, deep down, I worshipped his income and the life it provided more than I loved him. Would I *really* follow Curt wherever the Lord asked him to go? Even if that meant giving up everything we had worked so hard to attain?

If Curt did struggle with those questions, he didn't need to any longer. I was on board. I had released him from his role as provider, knowing that God could provide for our family in a way that my husband could not. I knew, when he took on the role in community ministry, that this was the kind of work he was born to do. And I wanted him to spend the rest of his life doing it. Now we knew the reason why Curt was born. And knowing that, I no longer wanted him to pursue a career. I wanted him to answer his calling.

Chapter 4

THE DECISION TO GO

Sometimes God Reveals His Will in Steps

I was so taken with the photo of Curt on-site, doing what he was born to do. With the words of Isaiah 26:3 in mind, I sent him a half-joking email.

"Hey, I can sell the house and save you the long trip home. You belong there. The kids and I will come over and meet you. Your picture says it all. No dark circles under your eyes. You look like a different person. We *must* make a change and the sooner, the better. The peace in your eyes and on your face is palpable. I am serious when I say I wish we could just meet you there. It gives me great peace and great happiness to have seen that picture."

I'm definitely a feeler, but Curt is a thinker. He is a person who doesn't make quick decisions or major changes based on emotion. Here is his response: "I don't believe my place is here beyond the next month. It is apparent that they would like me to stay in some capacity, but I don't see that really working. To be honest, they can't handle another worker with a family here. Especially one in which none of us knows the language, culture, and is brand new to this kind of work.

Trust me, I know a change is due and near and I'm lifting that up every moment and asking for guidance. I'm probably more anxious about it than you are. Can you imagine what it will be like when I return? As with everything else, as proven by how I got here in the first place, the path will be revealed in time so long as I'm obedient."

I sensed that he might need a little more encouragement, something I'm always happy to supply. So I replied.

"I understand. When I saw your picture, it just really hit me. You look like a different person. In a wonderful way. You look so peaceful and happy and like all is right with your world. No, I cannot imagine at all what it will be like for you when you get back, because now this life doesn't fit you anymore. You can't go back to how things were before you left. I won't let you. J It has been only two weeks and look at what God has already done! Look at all the proposals you have written, the construction, the relationships, the experiences, in just 2 weeks? It's unbelievable!

"...Know that I *fully* support you and I will go whenever and wherever God leads you, so take any concerns about me out of the equation. When I read your emails, my thoughts are 'wow, this is so amazing. This is so *you*. This is where you are meant to be and what you are meant to do'."

One of the highlights of Curt's initial six weeks was signing a contract on behalf of the NGO (non-government organization) that he represented to build homes for people who had lost everything in the earthquake and tsunami. In another email he wrote:

"I have signed contracts to buy homes for us in the States 5 times over the last 20 years and as happy as we were each of those times to be buying a home, none of those compare to what I just experienced. This is the first of about 80 homes we will build in this village. Brick, 2 bedroom, running water, electricity, kitchen, living room. For

$7,500. I'm in awe of the honor I just had. I'm still in shock over how things played out. I hadn't expected to play a role like this. The community where we will build got together and chose who would get the first house. Very cool."

Curt could see that the permanent team on the ground was being overworked and overstressed and was close to burn-out. They had been working nonstop since the tsunami six months before, and many of them had young children.

Several team members had helped with body removal in the initial months after the tsunami. Day after day they did nothing other than locate and remove corpses. The stench of death was still in the air six months later, and forever on their mind. Many of the team members were not eating or sleeping regularly because they were so overwhelmed with the magnitude of all that needed to be done. None of them had prior experience working in the aftermath of a disaster quite like this one. And sadly, few of them had had any experience working on a functional, healthy team. Curt felt like they needed someone to lead them in discussions to help make the transition from immediate relief work to long-term community development projects.

Although he had initially been sent to write project proposals, because of his age, experience, and gentle, wise nature, it was clear that Curt's role was becoming one of coach, facilitator, and consultant. And although he was working in accordance with his giftings, and quickly becoming a valued member of the team, he still was not feeling called to long-term work there.

I was frustrated. Curt was having the time of his life, and yet he was not yet willing to commit to it long-term. Maybe he didn't think I could give up all that I had for life in a nation with a culture so foreign to ours. And the kids. How would two kids who had been raised in an upper-middle-class home react to living in the Third World?

Working overseas on a short-term basis was one thing. But I suspected Curt was wondering if this could work long-term for his family.

Before he left the island, the team leader asked him to write a job description for the person who would fill his vacancy on the team. No one knew it at that time, but a year later Curt would return to Southeast Asia to fill that position. And this time he would bring along his family.

∞

On July 17, 2005, Curt came home a changed man. I could see it even from a distance at Raleigh-Durham International Airport. He looked tired from the thirty-plus-hour journey, but relaxed, happy, and excited about life. I couldn't remember the last time I had seen him this way.

Curt was burning with passion and purpose. He was finding what it meant to be the man God created him to be, doing the work God intended for him to do. He was discovering these things possibly for the first time in his life, and it showed.

He arrived home on a Saturday and returned to work the following Monday, despite being exhausted and having to deal with a twelve-hour time difference. As he pulled into his reserved parking space outside a sleek, high-tech office building, he was flooded with the immediate realization that he no longer fit here. After eighteen years with a company that had earned national recognition for its top benefits and stimulating and comfortable work environment, he no longer belonged. He was so overwhelmed that he couldn't walk through the front door. Instead, he took the back stairs to his office and closed the door.

The man who had left America six weeks earlier was gone. The job that had once consumed him now seemed relatively unimportant. The things that we worked so hard to obtain became trivial in light of all that Curt had experienced on the other side of the world. We knew we could no longer continue to live in the same way. After much praying, talking together, and discussing it with our pastor, J. D., we knew the next step to take. It was time for our whole family to put our "yes" on the table. We were willing to answer "Yes, Lord" to the call of Jesus.

Once our family was certain of what we were to do next, Curt sent a text message to the team leader in Southeast Asia. He said, in typical humble Curt fashion: "Hey dude, if you were really serious about me coming back long term and bringing my family, I'd like to talk to you about that."

We didn't know when or if the text would be replied to, as communication to that part of the world was still unreliable following the disaster. It could take days. Maybe the message hadn't even gone through. All we could do was wait. But within the hour we got this response: "Curt that is exactly the answer that we have been praying for. How soon can y'all get here?"

Chapter 5

UNDOING A LIFE

Preparing to Leave the Only Life We'd Ever Known

Once we made the initial commitment to move forward, Curt and I began talking about when and how we would share our decision with our children, Jordan and Molly. They were fourteen and ten at the time, and we had always discussed big and small decisions together. Our children knew that their dad had an important job at a major software company. They knew he had taken a big leap of faith by going to Southeast Asia. They were proud of him and knew that he was passionate about following God.

But did they understand all the ways this would affect their lives? The only times our children had been out of the country were for vacations in London and Paris. First-world, luxurious, cosmopolitan cities were no preparation for moving to a densely populated, traditional Muslim culture.

Jordan was in his freshman year of high school. Because we had moved frequently over the years, he had attended four elementary schools between kindergarten and fifth grade. The only consistency he'd had in his life, other than his immediate family, was the last three years of middle school, when he had stayed at the same school and lived in the same house. Change was a part of his life, and he was good at it.

Because I was an employee of the Chapel Hill-Carrboro City Schools, I was able to apply for Jordan to attend the newer of the two high schools, the one that had a better reputation and where his best friend would be. So when he started school that fall, he only knew one other student. A talented trumpet player, Jordan auditioned for and was accepted into the symphonic band. He was active in the youth ministry at The Summit. He was a good kid, never in trouble. Our biggest battle had to do with the kind of music he listened to. He was interested in the bands that Curt and I had liked when we were teen-agers: Van Halen, Pink Floyd, Led Zeppelin, among other less-than-edifying groups. We didn't want him listening to that music, as hypocritical as it sounds! Musical tastes aside, he did well in school and was a polite, sweet, sincere young man who was well liked. We knew that, compared to other families, we had it easy with Jordan.

Our daughter, Molly, was in fifth grade, in the same school and in the same wing of the building where I worked as a teacher assistant. I loved going to school with my daughter and catching a hug when we would pass each other in the hallways. Molly was a ballet dancer who, even though she was only ten, knew that she had found her life's passion and calling. She performed in a local production of *The Nut-cracker* every December and took classes several days a week in ballet and jazz. She was talented. She too was involved in student ministry at The Summit and was thriving in a small group for girls her age. Molly was a strong student as well, and was well liked by her teachers and classmates.

Though we had only lived there for five years, Chapel Hill was home to my kids, and Curt and Jordan were avid Tarheels fans. Like most residents of Chapel Hill, they loved college basketball. One of their favorite activities was to attend Late Night with Roy, the official start to the season. They would head to the Smith Center on the UNC campus to this free event for fans. They could watch the team at its first practice of the season, which would begin at midnight on the day deemed the official start to the year by the NCAA.

Curt loved taking Jordan and Molly to breakfast on Saturday mornings at Ye Olde Waffle Shop on Franklin Street while I slept in. And our family enjoyed watching Jordan play his trumpet in the annual Chapel Hill Town Holiday Parade. We loved our life in the town known as "the Southern part of heaven."

When your life is running as well, and as smoothly, as ours was, the thought of uprooting everything and starting from scratch in what could prove to be a hostile culture was unsettling, to say the least. It was one thing for Curt and me to be willing to step off the cliff and follow God, but what does it look like when you step off holding your child's hand? Especially a teenager. Would they hate it there and then resent us forever? We were going to ask them to walk away from the only life they had known, a life where they were thriving.

We decided it was better to tell them sooner rather than later. It was only fair to give them as much time as possible to prepare for what would come.

As Curt reviewed the chain of events, from his initial work locally in community ministry to the phone call letting him know that he was *exactly* the person they were looking for, we talked about what the six weeks apart had been like for Curt, and for the rest of us. We remembered how good God had been to all of us, and how our perspective had changed so that the only life that made sense was a life fully surrendered to and obedient to God.

We felt like when Curt went to Southeast Asia we had uncovered a huge, hidden secret that revealed a lie we all had lived with. Everything that our culture taught us about success, what it looks like, how to get it, and what it will give you was one big lie. We now saw that for us, it was just the opposite. It wasn't in the obtaining but in the releasing that we found meaning, purpose, and therefore, success. Together we were willing to go where God led, and do whatever He asked. There would be no holding back.

Curt explained that God was asking him to return to the island nation where he had served for six weeks. But this time God wanted him to return with our family, most likely in less than a year. When he asked our kids what they thought about it, Jordan spoke first.

"OK, well I have two questions. One, will I be homeschooled? Because that would be really cool. And two, Dad, can I help you in your work there?"

That was it. Once he knew the answers were yes and yes, his only response was "OK, cool."

Curt and I were overwhelmed at the depth of his trust in God and in us.

Our daughter, who had just been told by her dance instructor that she was "talented enough to go as far as she wanted in dance," was now hearing that she would be moving to a part of the world where there was no ballet. She simply said, "OK."

There were no more questions, just willing submission. We knew that both children were not just responding to us, but to God.

Although we had suspected that the kids would take the news well, I hadn't anticipated such a mature response. As usual, I was carrying around more guilt than I should have. Why had I assumed that the life we had was as good as it gets, that somehow in making this move we were asking our children to live with less? Why didn't I have the faith to believe that this could be the best thing we had ever done for them?

Probably because everything in me was a little scared. It's never easy to leave behind all that is familiar to you, knowing you are going to a place where hardly anything will come easily. And there was a second voice, this one came from the culture we live in.

Christian culture in America tells us that marriage and family is our number-one responsibility until the kids are grown. We are further told that the shakiest time in childrearing is the teenage years. I had heard enough stories to know that the teen years were supposed to be a nightmare, full of rebellion and danger and mounting problems. Most "good" parents would never uproot their kids at this stage of life. I was going to move my kids where for their middle school and high school years?

We don't have to hunt around for guilt. It's there for the taking. Admittedly, Jordan and Molly's immediate willingness to go made it a lot easier to take such a huge leap of faith. Still, I had to address the struggles I was dealing with.

The team leader back in Southeast Asia asked Curt how soon we could get there, and we foolishly thought we could leave in sixty to ninety days. It seemed so urgent that we get there as quickly as possible. They really needed us, and we were anxious to embrace the new life God was calling us to lead. And now that Curt had committed to going, he didn't want to spend another day working at SAS. We felt like a delay in our departure would be a waste of time.

We tried to make a list of everything we needed to do to prepare to leave. We had a 3,000-square-foot, fully furnished house and two cars to sell. Though we had moved many times in twenty-plus years of marriage, and were by no means pack rats, we had nevertheless accumulated some stuff.

We had friends we would leave, a church we wouldn't be able to take with us, jobs to resign from, and activities that our kids needed to finish out. We had to learn how to homeschool two kids who had been in traditional schools all their lives. We had immunizations to get for diseases we had never heard of, decisions to make about what to take with us, what to put in storage, and what to sell. We had a will to write. If we were not absolutely certain this was what God was calling us to do, it would have very quickly become much too overwhelming of a task.

Then there was the matter of telling people. We decided to share the news with just a few people. After all, Curt still had a job to keep so we could have a house to live in as we worked out the details of leaving. We told J. D. about our plans, and he advised us to apply to a large organization that was experienced in sending workers overseas. That way, we'd have the assistance and support of people who, unlike us, knew everything that is required for a successful transition. This turned out to be incredibly wise advice. This organization would train us and serve as our employer, pay our salary, supply our benefits, and assist us with important details such as securing a visa to work overseas.

As we looked into employment with this organization, we realized we faced a long application and approval process. It would be at least a year before we would be able to leave the States, and then only if we were accepted as employees and approved to go. We felt like we had hit a wall. The organization had a reputation for scrutinizing every detail of your life, and having very high standards and strict policies about who they would accept. Although it was comforting to know we would be backed by a world-class organization, we did not feel equipped or qualified. Immediately, doubts that I thought I had taken care of came back.

"Ha! You? They don't want someone like *you*. Wait until they find out your parents are divorced. Wait until they find out you were raised as a Catholic. You can kiss Curt's dream goodbye. He won't get to go because you have a past."

We filled out more and more paperwork and had more and more interviews, which did nothing to allay my fear that we would be rejected. But we weren't. Doors kept opening. Exceptions were made, like the fact that the organization was wary of sending a family with teenagers overseas. And despite the rumors we had heard, the organization was not looking for perfect people. If that was the standard, there would be no applicants.

It didn't matter that I had grown up Catholic, what mattered was that I had made a personal decision to give my life over to Christ many years before and I had a strong relationship with Him. Still, the approval process seemed to take forever. It was hard to be patient, especially for Curt, who could not wait to get back to work on the island.

Then, after almost a year-long application and approval process, we got the call offering us employment. But on that day, we were unable to accept their offer. My husband had gone in for a routine colonoscopy. Because his mother had died at fifty-two of colon cancer, my husband had been screened regularly since he was thirty years old. On that day, as we left the outpatient clinic, the doctor said to me, "Now it is important that Curt not make any important, life-changing decisions for the next twenty-four hours because of the anesthesia."

Since Curt was otherwise feeling well, we went from the doctor's office out to lunch and then stopped at Cold Stone Creamery to have ice cream with our kids. It was at Cold Stone that we got the call offering us the job. I laughed and explained our situation to the person who had called, saying that Curt would formally accept the position the next day.

We know now that as hard as it was to wait out that year, we had forgotten, or just in our arrogance refused to acknowledge, that we had a lot to learn before we would be ready to live and work overseas. God was continually growing us, teaching us, and preparing us in ways we never could have imagined that we needed.

Chapter 6

UNDER ATTACK

Choose to Follow God and You Will Experience Spiritual Warfare

As much as we wanted to get to Southeast Asia, we realized we needed to go through the year-long process of undoing our lives in the States and preparing for what was ahead. But as soon as we began submitting to the process, we started experiencing what can only be described as spiritual attack.

I'll make a confession. Although I had been a Christian for many years, it was not until we started making plans to go overseas that I became sensitive to spiritual warfare. We had been dealing with the reactions of people who questioned why a couple in their forties would walk away from a lucrative income and a comfortable lifestyle to live in a place most of our friends had never heard of. Answering those questions had not been difficult, but confronting the attacks of Satan was another thing entirely.

How do you explain to friends that Satan is doing all he can to keep you comfortable in North Carolina? I'm not exaggerating when I say people think you have lost it.

Spiritual warfare is real. It didn't end with the early church, nor is it limited to Christians who work in primitive cultures or areas where animism and paganism are the prevailing religions. In our lives, in our communities, there absolutely *is* a battle going on between good and evil. And when you are someone who is walking in obedience, dedicating your life to seeing the gospel transform people's lives, you instantly become Satan's adversary. He tags you as his number-one enemy.

Previously we had not been sensitive to this, so now I wonder if, in my commitment to a life of comfort and security, I had not posed much of a threat to Satan. He loves people who live for themselves and he wants them to stay that way. And that is what we had been doing, despite wanting to think otherwise.

Now we were under attack. It began in subtle ways, starting with lingering thoughts in the back of my mind. They sounded very much like this: "Are we *crazy*? What in the world are we doing? Is this just a mid-life crisis? What must people think of us?"

The "what ifs" can make you go nuts if you indulge them, and they make you question everything you are doing and everything you think you have heard from God. I would ask myself, *Hilary, are these kinds of thoughts from God? Clearly not.*

That sounded very convincing in my head. And if I could convince myself that easily, I assumed the thoughts were harmless. I'd just ignore them and they'd eventually go away. But my heart was not in line with my thinking. I was still struggling. After all, what we were doing went against everything our culture says is rational, sensible, safe, and secure. I felt like we were jumping off a cliff, banking everything on the promise that a net that we couldn't see would somehow catch us.

I started debating with God. "OK God, you said jump so I'm

gonna jump. You're gonna catch me, right? You're not going to let me fall off the edge and look stupid, right? Because everyone is saying that jumping off a cliff is really dumb. Especially when you have kids. And some people think it's not just dumb, but it's also selfish and irresponsible."

I had to remind myself of what I knew to be true. I kept coming back to the fact that God is God and I'm not. If I really do believe what I say I believe, that God is completely trustworthy, then why am I worrying like this? Isn't that the essence of obedience? When we are in our rightful place and God is in His, and we believe that every one of God's promises is true, it is only then that we are free to go wherever He tells us to go and do whatever He tells us to do. We can do that because we know that, without question, He is trustworthy.

Despite all the opposition and obstacles, walking forward in obedience was easy for us, simply because we believed that all of God's promises are true. And through it all, God was whispering: "Just trust me. I know what I'm doing."

Battling your own doubts and worries is one thing, but listening to others challenge your decision is something very different. I mentioned already that Christians tend to question the wisdom of uprooting children and moving them overseas. But the comments of some went deeper than that and had a greater impact on our thinking. Even to the point of damaging our hearts.

One of the only times I have seen my husband cry as a result of emotional pain was following a phone conversation with a close family member. Curt had told this relative what we were being called to do. Instead of hearing encouragement and support, and being asked to share more details about our plans, the relative joined the opposition.

This man had been a lifelong employee of the same organization, beginning right after his college graduation. He prides himself on being financially savvy and was considered "the smart one" in my husband's family. Upon hearing our news he told my husband he was an idiot. That is a direct quote. How could Curt quit his job to move to an unsafe, underdeveloped part of the world? He said to Curt: "People die there."

When you hear such words from a close family member, someone you love, admire, and respect, someone who has known you your entire live, it leaves a mark. But we knew you can't second-guess a decision to follow God because of input from someone who finds his security in his employment, income, and finances. And you can't compare the regions of the world where an oil company executive might be sent to the places where God calls his children to serve Him.

I guess our relative doesn't realize that people die in America, too, and all over the developed world.

It was a painful conversation, but it was a reminder that we didn't need other people's approval to follow where God was leading. Approval, no. But support and encouragement, yes. That would have been nice.

We received that type of response from a few members of our extended families. And beyond the positive words of some friends and relatives, God knew how to encourage us through His Word and His people. After we had made the decision to return to Southeast Asia as a family, J. D. preached a sermon series: The Friend of God: A Study of the Life of Abraham. The first sermon was " based on Genesis 12:1–3.

> Now the Lord said to Abram, "Go from your country and your
> kindred and your father's house to the land that I will show you.
> And I will make of you a great nation, and I will bless you and
> make your name great, so that you will be a blessing. I will bless

those who bless you, and him who dishonors you I will curse, and
in you all the families of the earth shall be blessed."

What comfort there was in knowing that long before we were born,
from the beginning of time, God was already doing with others exactly what He was doing in our lives. From the time of Abraham, He
has been calling ordinary people out, away from their home and everything familiar, and asking them to follow Him. He does this not to
destroy their lives, but with the intention of using us for His glory and
His purposes. God asked Abraham to "Go from your country...to the
land that I will show you." All that was required of Abraham was all
that God was asking of us—faith and obedience. Though the times
have certainly changed, our stories are the same.

God knew we needed to hear this sermon series. And what better
way to encourage us than through His Word! One Sunday during this
series, J. D. talked about surrender. He had us hold out our hands with
our palms facing up. He told us to visualize what was most important
to us, what we'd be willing to die for.

My immediate response? I would die for my husband and
children.

"Now," J. D. said, "squeeze your hands with the amount of firm-
ness representing how much you want to hold on to whatever you vi-
sualized in your hands." My knuckles turned white because these were
the people who meant more to me than anything!

Then J. D. said, "If you are willing to give whatever it is in your
hands to the Lord, regardless of what that means for you, then you
open your hands, again, palms facing up and say, 'Lord, they are yours,
do with them what you will because I release them to you. They're not
mine anyway. They are yours'."

Although this may seem like a very simple (and maybe even a little bit cheesy) exercise, it ended up being significant for me. And just at the right time. I was literally letting go, not just of our jobs and possessions, but of the control I mistakenly thought I had over my children's lives. I was setting aside the hope and security I had put in my husband. I was saying that I would trust God to care for us, instead of the earthly things that I used to put my trust in. I needed to release my desire for control. I needed to find in God all of my security, my hope, and my confidence. No longer could I rely on my role as a mother, and certainly not in my husband and his career.

At a time when Satan was attacking all of my insecurities, all of my feelings about being a good parent, the Lord spoke to me: "Go… to the land that I will show you" (Genesis 12:1. For us, that land was a beautiful but dark island in Southeast Asia.

"And your ears shall hear a word behind you, saying, This is the way, walk in it" (Isaiah 30:21.

We were willing and ready. But as we continued to make preparations to leave, the attacks intensified. It was clear that when God sends someone out in His name, that person becomes Satan's number-one enemy.

We knew the occasional nerves we felt about selling our possessions, the questions that lingered in our minds, were not from God, they were from the enemy. We reminded ourselves almost daily that we belonged to God, and we were answering the call that He had put on our lives. We had to keep moving forward in obedience because we were certain who was leading us. We had to continually remind ourselves that because we belonged to God, Satan had no authority over us.

Chapter 7

SELLING IT ALL

Letting Go of the Accessories of a "Perfect Life"

As the months went by, we began the process of selling our assets and possessions. I enjoyed decorating and creating a homey, comfortable environment for my family. I confess that I had been on a constant quest to find things that would make our home feel perfect.

My parents divorced when I was in college, and when I think about the home I grew up in, many of my memories are that it was a stressful and unhappy place. I have no childhood memories of home being a sanctuary. So I was determined to provide a completely different kind of home for my children. That made our home important to me, far beyond being just the house we lived in. But I now realized that my house and its contents stood in the way of our ability to leave for overseas, and I was ready to part with things. Or so I thought.

We decided to first sell the upholstered furniture, knowing it wouldn't store well while we were away. The first item I sold was a wonderful, sage green, chenille club chair and ottoman that I had bought from the upscale store, Restoration Hardware. It had down cushions and soft fabric, the perfect chair to sink into with a book! And though I had gone the less costly route and bought it off the floor, it was still expensive. Back then I was obsessed with comfort. I wanted all my furniture to feel wonderful and relaxing. I wanted my family to see our home as a refuge from the busy life we were living.

I sold the chair and ottoman on Craig's List for seventy-five dollars, at least ninety percent less than what I paid for it. When I sold it, all I could think was *Oh my, what are we doing?* I even cried a little, as I wondered if we would ever again be able to afford to buy a chair.

I started to have doubts.

Is this crazy? We aren't young and foolish, we're in our forties! We have kids! What if we can never afford to buy a house again? And what if we can? How in the world will we be able to furnish it if we sell all our stuff?

I had never had a panic attack before, but I felt like this time I just might.

As our possessions started heading out the door, I realized something that made me feel ashamed. I had wasted so much time searching and shopping for the perfect things for my perfect house in the perfect subdivision. I had spent money on so many things that now were completely worthless to me. I had wasted so much time taking care of and worrying about my things. Suddenly I felt ashamed because I couldn't get any of that time back. And now, none of this carefully selected and cared-for stuff mattered. I couldn't wait to get rid of stuff that had been so important to me.

These realizations were necessary, and I found that God had even more to teach me.

When I began to see possessions for what they were, nothing more than a bunch of *stuff,* I realized that in unloading it all I hadn't actually given up anything. Others referred to us as "the family that gave up everything." I hated hearing that because although people meant well, it just wasn't true. We weren't losing in any way, because once we started to let go of things I started to see that we were actually gaining.

As we sold off our possessions, I finally began to feel free! That's right, in letting go I gained freedom from the bondage that was my stuff! I hadn't realized how much all these things had tied me down until I let them go.

The last item I sold was an antique dining room table and chairs, something I had spent months searching for. I probably visited dozens of antique stores all over North Carolina searching for just the one. When I finally found it, I ended up getting really ripped off. I had become so obsessed with finding just the right table that I paid too much for it. As a result, I ended up hating the table and chairs.

Looking back on it, I realized that we sat around that overpriced table only once or twice in all the time we had it. So the result of all the time I wasted looking and all the money I spent was having to walk past a table that I ended up barely using, not liking at all, and completely regretting. Although it looked beautiful, every time I walked past that table I felt stressed. I couldn't wait to have it out of my life. It had been one big, expensive mistake.

I sold it to a woman who said, "Oooh I am so happy. Now when my children and grandchildren come to dinner we can all sit around one table." And rather than having a sinking feeling in the pit of my stomach over selling it at a fraction of what I had paid for it, this time I could smile and say with complete confidence: "That's great! Take it! I hope you love it!" My stuff just didn't matter to me anymore.

God was giving me a lot of peace about the huge transition we were going through. Despite how I felt when the selling-off process had started, over time my feelings and perspective changed completely.

Not only was I at peace about letting go of everything, it was an incredibly freeing thing to not own anything. It was definitely weird and felt rather radical and a little irresponsible, especially at my age. But it was so *freeing*.

I realized finally how weighed down I had been by stuff. This is one of the great secrets in life: the possessions we think give us a sense of security lie to us. They weigh us down, steal our affections, stress us out, and waste our time and money. In all these ways, they lie to us. And it is in letting go of them that we actually feel secure and free and at peace.

The day after we sold our house, our cars, and most of our possessions, we were sitting at a bus stop in downtown Chapel Hill. It's hard to describe the feeling of waiting at a bus stop knowing you have no home, no car, and few possessions. I started to giggle because there we were, two adults in their forties with a then-eleven-year-old and a fifteen-year old, all of whom were thankful that our town had free public transportation. We had no transportation of our own, but I have never felt so free.

Picture yourself being able to say and experience the following: "We don't owe anyone any money for anything! We aren't tied down because of a job or a house or possessions or the responsibility to maintain anything! We can do anything and go anywhere!"

I was so excited, I felt like I never wanted to own anything again! One of our friends started to understand some of what we were so happy about. She said, "Wow, it must be great not to have any debt. It must be a very free feeling."

Indeed it was. Being free of any worldly debt! What a picture, I realized, of my standing with God. It wasn't just that my financial state was debt-free, my life was as well. When you give your life over to Christ, the debt we are all in before God because of our sin is paid *in full.* That is where our only real sense of freedom can come from. It didn't take our preparing to move to the other side of the world to experience that. It just took the surrender of our hearts and our plans to God.

Chapter 8

And Then the Struggle

*Attacks from Satan That Force
Us to Question Everything*

It took us a full year to undo our life in North Carolina so we could leave the country. We found it to be hard on every level. As we went through the application process with our sending organization, Curt continued working for SAS. We were still living in our house and had a mortgage to pay. At age forty-three, he had finally discovered his calling and couldn't wait to get started. Yet he was still enmeshed in the life we were leaving behind, working in a stressful position. He struggled during that time with two conflicting roles he had to play: IT director and aspiring cross-cultural worker.

But he kept at it because he wasn't confident that if he revealed his plans to resign and move overseas, that SAS would keep him on until we were ready to move. Can you imagine walking into a vice president's office and giving a year's notice, acknowledging that you have no intention of ever coming back, but asking to be kept on the payroll?

Almost two years before Curt's initial trip to Southeast Asia, SAS acquired another business on the West Coast. This newly acquired company had a division that functioned similar to the one that Curt managed in North Carolina. As a result, Curt saw the need for a major reorganization to consolidate the two groups.

He began travelling between North Carolina and the West Coast, attending a series of contentious meetings to put the wheels in motion to merge the two groups. The head of the West Coast division was a driven woman whose position and title were clearly the foundation of her identity, and she was not about to go down without a fight. Curt's proposal that the two divisions be merged under his leadership became a bi-coastal battle. After months of silence, top management in North Carolina decided that it wasn't the right time for such a merger. Nevertheless, the discussions and tension between Curt and this woman continued for more than a year.

I had always admired Curt's ability to think and act in the best interests of the company, without skewing things to advance his own career. And this potential merger was no different. Curt worked hard to position the move as a strategic blending of resources with huge potential for growth and increased productivity. Why maintain two separate divisions doing the same thing on opposite sides of the country when employees from the West Coast could be transferred to North Carolina, bringing expertise that was missing at corporate headquarters?

Although the merger, if approved, would mean a huge promotion for Curt, with increased responsibility and an increase in salary, his motivation was to help SAS do better business. He knew it was the right thing to do.

And then he went to Southeast Asia for the first time, being out of the office for six weeks. When he came home, what he had been advocating for at work suddenly didn't matter to him anymore. Rather than fighting his way to the top, Curt proposed that the details of the merger be worked out, minus the decision of who would lead the new organization. He convinced his vice president that the most important thing was to decide how resources would be allocated. Naming the head of the new division could be done later, because while he still wanted the merger to come through he knew that his resignation would be coming soon. He would never lead the new division he had fought for.

We felt like we were going about things the right way, being systematic about settling the details of our life so we would be free to leave without loose ends. But Satan knows the things that will trip us up, and he unleashed a big one about a month before Curt submitted his resignation. There had always been one area of our shared life where we had looked for a sense of security and worth, and that was our income. Curt knew he was leaving SAS, and he planned to tender his resignation in four weeks. And that was when he was offered the huge promotion he had worked for and wanted for so long.

All his hard work, the cross-country flights, the stress of the many contentious meetings, the sleepless nights would have suddenly seemed worth it. His recommendations would be accepted by senior management, and he would be rewarded with a higher level of responsibility. Before his first trip to Southeast Asia, he would have jumped at the offer of a higher position. Now, he wasn't even tempted. We knew that placing our trust and security in companies, careers, and incomes was the opposite of putting our trust in a completely reliable God. The empty feeling Curt had when he was offered the promotion was another confirmation that we were absolutely doing the right thing.

The timing of the offer made us laugh. We knew it was a deliberate attempt by the enemy to get us to turn our backs on God's call. I remember thinking, *Nice try, Satan. Can't you do any better than that?*

When the lure of a promotion failed to distract us, Satan interfered in our lives in a way that went straight to the heart. He attacked our oldest child.

∞

Our last summer in the States was winding down and we decided to have a yard sale to sell off the remainder of our belongings. The night before the yard sale, our fourteen-year-old son, Jordan, had a fever and went to bed early. We had friends over, and when Jordan chose to stay in bed rather than joining the festivities I knew he was really sick. We assumed it was just a virus that would pass after a good night's rest, but we could not have been more wrong. He woke up the following morning with his left eye swollen shut. He couldn't open it. We assumed he was having an allergic reaction and knew he needed immediate medical attention.

Curt drove him to a Doctor's Urgent Care while our daughter and I attended to our yard sale. Because the Lord is sovereign over all things, we now know why Curt had difficulty finding the clinic and ended up driving an hour out of his way. For someone who can navigate in any city, it was unusual that he got that lost. (This was before we all had a GPS in our car.)

As Curt and Jordan searched for the Urgent Care, our son's condition worsened, so that by the time they arrived his case was taken seriously. When a doctor came to examine him, Jordan was vomiting repeatedly from the pressure that was building behind his eye. He had never been one to complain when he was sick, but this time he was telling Curt, "I'm in agony, Dad."

The doctors were perplexed, not knowing if it was an infection, an allergic reaction, or something else. Curt was calling to give me updates as I tried to hold the yard sale. Jordan was in excruciating pain, his eye was still swollen shut, and he was continually vomiting. Curt was worried, and it came through in his phone calls.

Just two weeks earlier, Curt and Jordan had returned home from a two-week mission trip to Botswana where they had slept in tents, eaten out of the back of a truck, and worked in AIDS clinics. I began to wonder if there might be a relationship between my son's illness and something he was exposed to overseas. I asked Curt, "Have you told them he was in Africa two weeks ago? I wonder if that might be relevant."

The news that he had been in Africa working with AIDS patients changed everything. This could be something much more serious than a possible allergic reaction. As Jordan's condition worsened, Curt called and asked that I come immediately to the clinic. I closed down the yard sale, and because we were without a car I asked a neighbor to drive me and Molly. As soon as I saw my son I was shocked by his deteriorating condition. The doctors directed us to the Emergency Room at University of North Carolina Hospitals. I'll never forget the urgency of their words: "We need you to drive to the ER *immediately*. You will get there faster in your car than if we call for an ambulance. When you get there, do *not* let them make you wait."

As we helped our groaning, still-vomiting son into the car, the nurse that was assisting us mentioned that she was a member of The Summit church. It was reassuring to know that we had that connection, that even in the clinic parking lot God was putting His people alongside us.

Though the waiting room in the ER at UNC Hospital was full, we were seen immediately. Test after test was run and an endless stream of medical professionals—nurses, radiologists, ophthalmologists, pediatricians, infectious disease specialists, ER doctors—came in and out of the room. They all were trying to determine what was happening—and to do it as quickly as possible. As he writhed in agony, Jordan smiled faintly and whispered: "Don't worry, Mom, I can still praise God in this storm." Then he squeezed my hand.

While my frighteningly ill son tried to reassure me, I could see reason for even greater concern. The doctors huddled in the hallway outside, conferring. I kept hearing the words *Africa* and *AIDS,* as medical professionals tried to assess what might be happening. I have never felt so helpless and scared.

Finally, it was determined that Jordan had orbital cellulitis, a dangerous infection behind his eye. The infection was known to cause serious complications, including blindness. The infection had entered his bloodstream and was getting worse. The doctors said he was in danger of losing his eye, and the first twenty-four hours would be the most critical. He was admitted to the hospital and infused with five different antibiotics in a desperate attempt to bring the raging infection under control. We would know in a day if his eye would be spared.

Our son was hospitalized for five days. Our lives stood still during that time as we prayed, waited, and cared for Jordan in the hospital. Thanks to the quick intervention of the brilliant doctors at UNC, and the aggressive treatment they ordered, Jordan's eye and sight were saved.

Up to this point, we had been careful to watch what we said about our plans to move overseas, since we would be living in a strict Muslim province. We never told those outside of our sending agency exactly where we would be working. But seeing my son so critically ill, with the health of his eye in such danger, I stood in the hallway of UNC Hospital, looked the chief pediatrician in the eye, and said, "In October we'll be moving…" and I named the exact location of our new home in Southeast Asia.

Then the questions of a mother poured out of me. "Do you think that is a safe move for our son? Is there any risk for him in moving forward with our plans? Please tell me if there is and we will change the plan right now."

The pediatrician was quick to respond. "Your son will make a complete recovery. In a few months this will all be just a bad memory."

After five days in the hospital, where I joked with Jordan that he was the only patient in pediatrics who could grow a moustache, he was released. But the ordeal wasn't over.

Within hours of our arrival back home, a nurse came to visit and explained the process for continuing the antibiotics our son needed. The drug would be administered through a peripherally inserted central catheter, a PICC line. It is a form of IV access that was inserted in the bend of Jordan's arm running beneath the skin up to his heart. Curt and I would be administering a series of IV antibiotics every six hours, around the clock, for the next three weeks. Good thing we didn't fully understand all that this entailed until *after* we came home. Otherwise, I never would have left the hospital!

I tried not to panic when the nurse explained that if I didn't prepare the syringes a certain way, my son could get a life-threatening blood clot. Inside I was screaming at the nurse, who seemed way too matter-of-fact in her instructions. Didn't she realize how fragile and worn out I was?

Are you kidding me? I can't do this! What if I don't do it right? I just spent five days in the hospital not knowing if my son would come home blind, and now if I don't do this right I could jeopardize his life? I'm exhausted and scared.

Oh, and did I mention we are in the middle of preparing to move to a Third World country?

The nurse didn't back down. In fact, she was so "this is what you do, so go ahead and do it" about everything that her get-over-yourself approach forced me to believe I was capable of handling this. Maybe because I realized that I didn't have a choice. I wrote down everything I was supposed to do, step by step, knowing that no detail was minor.

I was so afraid I would make a mistake. Curt took my notes and typed them up. Every time we administered Jordan's medications, even the very last time, we double-checked our step-by-step instructions. We couldn't afford to make any mistakes.

Our life for those three weeks revolved around taking care of Jordan. Every time I opened our refrigerator, all I could see were syringes, which were delivered by the box full every few days. It made me want to cry. And yet, we had to maintain our composure so as not to alarm our children.

Curt and I moved the mattress from our bed into the second-floor family room and set up Jordan's bed in there as well. So for the last three weeks we lived in our Chapel Hill home, Curt, Jordan, and I slept in the same room, with Molly's room right across the hall.

Curt and I took turns administering Jordan's IV medications. Each round of meds would take about one hour to administer, so it was almost like having a newborn again. We were getting up in the middle of the night, every night. And because our son was attached to an IV all day long, he missed out on his last three weeks in North Carolina.

He missed going to church camp with his best friend, he missed going to the pool and doing all the normal things kids do during the summer. But the one thing he could do that made him feel like himself was play the guitar. We wanted him to have this outlet, even though every time he tried to play, blood would seep into the PICC line and we'd have to call a home nurse to come out and flush his line. So he stopped playing, simply because he didn't want to inconvenience the nurses. It was so discouraging to watch, and yet the only person who didn't seem upset about it was Jordan.

Most teenagers would have been depressed, discouraged, bored, frustrated, and angry at being practically tied to a bed for the last three weeks of summer. But not Jordan. Throughout the ordeal, he never complained. He was cheerful and even thanked us after every infusion. Every six hours for three weeks straight he thanked us. Through all of this God was teaching us: "It's not about just trusting me with your income and your stuff. Are you going to trust me with your kids' lives?"

Yes, we were.

Chapter 9

THE EMPTY KEYCHAIN

Laying Down What Once Seemed So Important

Once Jordan received a clean bill of health we were able to move forward with the final step before we could leave the States. The organization that was sending us overseas required that we spend seven weeks at an orientation and training facility in another state. The four of us would live at the facility in community with other individuals and families who were preparing to do what we were, although headed to a number of different countries. It was reassuring to meet so many like-minded people.

We went through orientation with people ranging in age from newly graduated from college to senior citizens. It was a great picture of the Body of Christ working together. I became so much more aware that we had been chosen for this task. God had selected us from the six billion people on earth that He could have recruited. That was amazing, empowering, and very humbling.

In the small, sparsely furnished apartment where we stayed during our training, I took out my now-empty key chain and hung it on the bulletin board in the kitchen. It had once been filled with car, house, and office keys. It was leather and had my initials embroidered on one side—a gift from the mother of one of my former fifth grade students. The empty key chain was a reminder of all that we had let go of and all that we had been through in the last week leading up to our arrival at training. The keys that had been so important in our former life had been replaced with "keys to the Kingdom." Namely, living in obedience to God's calling on our lives.

In the five days leading up to this final stage of preparation, our training, we had sold the last of our cars, sold our home, sold the rest of our belongings, took our son to a series of doctor appointments where the PICC line was finally removed. Curt had resigned his job of eighteen years, we put into storage what remained of our earthly goods (mostly things we want our children to have someday), tearfully gave our dog to her new family, taught our last Sunday school class, said goodbye to precious friends, and packed what little remained into a van to leave North Carolina. All that in just five days.

We thought we had come to the training facility to learn: to study the people we'd be serving, to learn about the culture we'd be entering, and more about the work we would be doing. And we did learn, but more importantly we grew in ways we didn't realize we needed to. Our minds expanded, yes, but our hearts were broken for those we'd not yet met and the lostness that covers the globe.

We learned in those seven weeks that we didn't need a house or a car or pots and pans or even our precious photo albums. We didn't need a key chain, empty or otherwise. We needed God leading us in our new life, we needed each other to walk this road together, and we needed our friends and our family to be behind us, praying with us and for us. It was in letting go of all of this that I realized the empty key chain didn't represent all we had given up, but rather that God had unlocked the secrets of the blessings that come when you step out in faith and walk in obedience with and toward Him.

We hadn't left the States yet and already He was showing me that I hadn't given up anything. Quite the opposite: I was gaining everything.

∞

Still, there were struggles. Most of them had little to do with giving up a familiar way of life. We were ready for that. But other aspects of our life, unrelated to career or achievement, were important to us. These were the things that we struggled to let go of.

Molly was eleven years old when we moved to Southeast Asia. She had been training in classical ballet since she was four, and it was becoming clear that this was not just a passion but a gift that God had given to her. At a young age, she knew exactly what she wanted to do when she got older. And now, at the age where her level of training should become much more intense, we were moving to a place where there would be no ballet.

At home in North Carolina, she was a member of a performing ballet company. She had been in the cast of *The Nutcracker* every December for three years, working her way up through the ranks. She was eight years old when she was cast as an angel. Through months of rehearsals, she would watch the older girls work on their solos. When it came time for the technical rehearsals at the theatre just before the show opened, she would scoot a chair up to the front of the audience seating, climb on top, and lean her chin on the stage to watch the senior girls. She would do this for hours, studying the older dancers' every move.

Ever since she had first performed in *The Nutcracker,* Molly had been anticipating the year that she would turn eleven, old enough to audition for a role she had always wanted, Clara. Now, because of our move, she would never get that audition. We were still in the States when the auditions were held without her.

We were moving in October, and that fall her ballet classmates were scheduled to get their first pair of pointe shoes. This is the day that every young ballet dancer dreams about. It's a huge rite of passage and Molly couldn't wait to get hers. Every year when she would dance in *The Nutcracker,* she would make friends with an older dancer who would allow a very thrilled Molly to try on her pointe shoes. In her young eyes, having pointe shoes was the great divide between aspiring dancers and serious, real ballet dancers.

Knowing we would not be here when her peers got their shoes, I asked one of her teachers if Molly could get hers early. I knew that if we moved to Southeast Asia without them, Molly would never be able to step back into ballet upon our return home. She would have missed years of training and strengthening that would make it very difficult to pick it back up again. The teacher agreed, so we bought her shoes and arranged for her to have private instruction. A natural dancer, Molly took to the pointe shoes immediately, able to pirouette after just a few hours.

∞

A few days before we were set to leave the country, Curt and I were speaking to a group from our church. One of the people in attendance asked about my feelings regarding moving my children to a strict Muslim culture. I talked about asking our daughter to lay down her ballet dreams and described her willing sacrifice in giving up her lessons. I talked about how it had been hard for me, as her mom, to ask her to do that given where she was in her training. I was getting choked up and, as I talked, I could see tears in the eyes of some of the mothers. When I was finished speaking, one of the men in the group raised his hand.

"You need to talk to my wife afterward. She's a dancer and she owns a dance studio. But she is so choked up right now she can't talk."

I couldn't believe it. My daughter's dream was one of the hardest things for me to let go of, and who was present but a dancer. Right away I knew that this was no chance encounter.

Afterward Curt and I talked with Jenn, and she told us about her dance career. At one time she had been told she would never dance again due to an injury, but God provided healing and she went on to have a long and successful career. Now she owned a studio. She was so supportive and encouraging, it was as if God was standing right in front of me saying, "I know how hard this is for you and how you are struggling with it. But it's OK, I know what I'm doing. Will you trust me with Molly's ballet? Will you trust me with her future?"

Molly was so excited to meet Jenn, a woman who could understand her heart. And I was so excited to have such tangible evidence that God really understood the deepest desires of my heart. He knew how to take care of even the smallest detail. I knew without a doubt that this meeting with Jenn was directly from Him.

A few days later, on the morning we were to leave for the airport, a woman I had never met delivered something to the home where we were staying. It was from Jenn.

She sent Molly two beautiful ballet tutus, the kind young girls dream about wearing onstage. She also sent a DVD of a ballet class, several CDs of barre music, including a description of what exercises to do with each piece of music, a ballerina ornament, a ballet charm bracelet and two precious letters that she wrote to Molly. These are the types of letters that you save for life.

In one of the letters, Jenn included a special ring. She explained that the ring had been given to her when she was just a little bit older than Molly. At that age, Jenn had been told by a doctor that she would never dance again as a result of an injury. At that time a friend gave her the ring as a reminder that she believed that Jenn would indeed dance again. And as I said earlier, Jenn was able to do everything with her career that she had dreamed of. Now, she was passing that same ring on to Molly. She wanted Molly to know that her dreams could come true.

I knew God had placed Jenn in our lives just as we were leaving to build us up when Molly and I were both unsure. God knew it was a struggle for us to see Molly have to walk away from ballet, and He was attending to some of our deepest fears. What a very personal reminder that even the things that seem relatively insignificant matter to God simply because they matter to us. What a wonderful picture of Jeremiah 29:11: "For I know the plans I have for you, declares the Lord, plans for wholeness and not for evil, to give you a future and a hope."

God knew Molly was laying down her life's dream for the sake of the gospel. And He knew that I was trusting Him as I asked my daughter to do that. That morning, through Jenn's thoughtfulness and generosity, the Lord was telling me and Molly, "Trust me. I know what I am doing and I know what you are laying down. I can and I will provide for you. Just trust me."

∞

With God's assurances fresh in our minds, it was time to go. I was not sad to leave America, the only home I had known. I was excited and ready for what lay ahead. But I did board the first of six flights that would take us to our destination with one deep and nagging concern: would I feel safe there?

We were going to live in one of the strictest Muslim areas in the world. And we were a family of white, western Christians. Islamic law was enforced in the province where we would be living, and conversion to Christianity could be punishable by death.

We all have seen news reports of the harshness of Shari'a law.

What if the locals found out what we were all about? Would they burn our house down? Would they threaten us and terrorize our children? Would we be able to make friends? What would it be like if everyone around us hated us for who we were?

I was very willing to go, but in my heart I felt that I had something to fear. This was not like heading out to serve in Western Europe or Latin America. As we traveled, I reminded myself that it was God who had called us to Southeast Asia. And for comfort, I repeated Bible verses:

"He who calls you is Faithful" (1 Thessalonians 5:24).

"Be strong and courageous and do it. Do not be afraid and do not be dismayed, for the Lord God, even my God, is with you. He will not leave you or forsake you" (1 Chronicles 28:20).

And those who know your name put their trust in you, for you, O Lord, have not forsaken those who seek you (Psalm 9:10.

"Fear not, for I am with you" (Isaiah 41:10).

"Sojourn in this land and I will be with you and I will bless you" (Genesis 26:3).

"God arms me with strength and he makes my way perfect" (Psalm 18:32).

These are just a few of the verses that brought me comfort by reminding me of what is true. I relied on statements of God's promises, strength, and love during a time when I was tempted to believe these things were not true.

After six flights and countless hours travelling, we arrived at our destination. I stepped out of the plane and took my first ground-level look at the city where we would live—on one of the most beautiful islands in the world. At that moment, all my fears were lifted and I immediately knew I was safe. That complete peace did not come over me until I had taken my first step on the ground of our new city. It was evening when we landed, so the sky was dark, but the atmosphere was silent and serene.[1]

There was a gentle breeze and though it was dark, I could see coconut trees and banana trees in the distance. Tropical beauty has always resonated deep in my soul. I loved my new city as soon as I took my first step onto its soil. I can only liken it to that instant connection, bond, and love you feel when you hold your children for the first time. It was love at first sight and peace at first step.

I knew this was going to be a safe place for my family. I knew God was giving me that peace, since I could not have done it on my own. It was the one thing I had been worrying about all along, and it was gone in an instant.

I knew that God would not call us to leave all we knew and then suddenly drop out of the picture just as we boarded the plane. We were still the same people, preparing to live where God had sent us. I gave Him my greatest fear and He gave me instant peace. When you know that you are exactly where God wants you to be, there is nothing to worry about.

---

1. Though relief money has since been allocated to rebuild, expand, and modernize the airport, at the time of our move I stepped out of the plane onto a portable metal staircase. In this region, there were no jetways. So my first step out of the plane took me immediately outdoors.

Chapter 10

CULTURE SHOCK

Learning Just How Faithful God Really Is

Culture shock is not an "if" but a "when" for people who live cross-culturally. Thankfully, we had been well-oriented during seven weeks of training in the States. We knew what to expect and which symptoms of culture shock to look for.

But here is the reality. No matter how well prepared you think you are, you aren't prepared. Otherwise, culture shock wouldn't be called a shock.

Of the four of us, Jordan was hit hardest. This came as a surprise because he has a laid-back temperament and is never one to complain. Just months before we left for Southeast Asia he spent a few weeks in Africa. He lived in tents in an impoverished area of Botswana and worked in AIDS clinics, and when he got home he said he couldn't wait to return to Africa. It was the first place he had ever been where he said, "I can't wait to go back." In contrast, when we would get back from a vacation, he would always say, "That was nice, but it's good to be home."

Jordan realized that Southeast Asia is no Africa. And a two-week trip is no comparison for planting your life somewhere for two to three years. About four weeks into our time there, after the honeymoon period had ended, he was flat-out miserable. Admittedly, he was dealing with a lot of changes all at once. The weather was oppressively hot, every day. And we knew it would be that way all year long. When we had running water at our house, we had to bathe and wash our hands and clothes in water that was not clean enough to drink. Frequently it smelled like rotten eggs. The electricity was inconsistent, and sometimes it was out all night, which made it impossible to sleep because we couldn't run a fan or air conditioner.

On top of the other adjustments, five times a day every day we heard the call to prayer blaring from loudspeakers at the mosque next door to our house. Also, every day, despite our best efforts to keep them at bay, we were bombarded by ants, cockroaches, and geckos, along with the occasional rat. Welcome to the tropics.

Whenever we went outside, Jordan saw his mother and sister have to cover themselves from head to toe despite the oppressive heat. Just to get to our car we had to skirt cows, chickens, and goats that would find their way into our front yard. And everywhere we went, local men gave Molly and me unwanted attention, which was stressful for Jordan because he felt like he should protect us. As if that weren't enough, he didn't have any American teenagers to hang out with, and because we were white we were stared at everywhere we went.

Every day we were hearing a language we didn't yet fully understand, eating strange and spicy food, and smelling smells that were new to us. Beggars came by our house almost every day asking for money, which got annoying after a while. Living in the Third World involves close contact with a lot of dirt and, without being seen, a lot of bacteria, which left us feeling queasy from time to time. It also gave us random illnesses and fevers, and every time we were sick we began to wonder if we had contracted dengue fever, malaria, typhoid, or parasites. When Jordan would try to find retreat in his room, something would inevitably disrupt his peace. It might be a scorpion crossing the floor, a sudden power outage that could last all day, an earthquake, which happened frequently, or noise from outside.

Like everyone who experiences culture shock, Jordan started to idolize America and he longed to return. We reviewed the list of symptoms of culture shock together. Questioning whether you made the right decision in moving, idolizing your home culture, loss of identity, trying too hard to absorb everything, irritability, anger, resentment, feeling overwhelmed or lost, suffering a lack of confidence. He showed signs of every one. I assured him again and again that he "wouldn't always feel that way," that this was a normal, temporary response to such a radical change in his life. I reminded him that God, who had called us *all* to go there, was faithful. We could trust God to bring him out of culture shock and we would stand beside him and encourage him through it. We needed to pray, to trust, and to be patient.

Still, he wasn't buying. So I asked him if there was anything at all that that he liked in our city.

"The beach," he said. "I like the beach,"

"OK, then," I said, "let's go right now. And we will go every day if we have to. Because you don't ever have to love it here, but by the time we leave I hope you will be able to say that you like it. And if going to the beach makes you happy, that's what we'll do."

Twenty minutes later we were staring at the Indian Ocean, marveling that this was where we got to *live*. We spent a lot of time at the beach when we first arrived, and truthfully that was a good thing. At the beach we could unwind and have what felt like an afternoon-long vacation. And with all the changes we were going through, we needed frequent breaks. It is physically, emotionally, and spiritually exhausting to live in such a radically different culture. Spending hours every day studying a new language was tiring. Adjusting to an oppressively hot climate was draining. One ex pat told me it would take a year before we would feel completely comfortable living there.

"A *year*?" I gasped. Surely it wouldn't take that long. But she was right, it did.

The beaches in our city were the most beautiful we had ever seen. On the northern tip of our island the water was so clear we could see our feet on the ocean floor. We enjoyed discovering different beaches and found that each one was different. One beach had soft white sand and another had terrific snorkeling, and they all had spectacular scenery.

In 2006 and even into 2007, we had the beaches to ourselves any time we went because the locals were avoiding the sea following the tsunami. Beach trips turned out to be a wonderful respite for our family, a place where we could relax, enjoy God's creation, enjoy one another, play, have some privacy, and finally be ourselves.

But we couldn't spend all our time relaxing on a beach. There were some nights when I was so concerned about Jordan's emotional and spiritual health that I slept in his room. The one time each day when he had to be alone, while he was sleeping, I wanted him to know that one of us was literally by his side.

Though I knew God had not moved us to the other side of the world to destroy my son, I wondered how and when Jordan would come out of culture shock. I had observed another western family living in country with children the same age as mine who lived in a city that was comparatively much easier to live in. Their city had movie theatres, Starbucks, and malls, and the locals were far less suspicious of outsiders. But even then, that family became so overwhelmed by culture shock that they returned to the States. Would that be us? I knew it wouldn't, but still I worried about our son, who was with us physically but was far from being entirely with us. I wanted him back.

Our family prayed constantly for Jordan, and it was hard when we didn't get the immediate answer we wanted. I wanted God to make all the pain and suffering go away, and I wanted it to happen *now*. I clung to what I knew was absolutely true—that God was faithful and that Jordan would be OK because God would see him through this valley.

Despite his feelings of wanting to go home, Jordan never gave up. Although at times he was miserable, he continued to put himself out there, trying everything that came his way. He was persevering through his pain, and I knew he would come out of it.

About six months into our time overseas, The Summit Church sent the first team of volunteers to work alongside us. On that team were two guys who had gone to Africa with Curt and Jordan the summer before. One was a dear man who became like a brother to Curt and a beloved uncle to Jordan, and the other was one of Jordan's best friends.

I think that was the turning point. When his friend came and he got to show him around and introduce him to his new life, he finally began to embrace it. I worried how Jordan would react when it was time for our friends to return to the States, but rather than wishing he could get on the plane, he was OK! He hugged his friend, thanked him for coming, and said, "I love you, brother."

Our son was content to remain behind with us. I knew then that he was embracing God's call on our family's lives and starting to bond with his new country.

Although it was a painful experience for all of us, my teenage son learned lessons for eternity by relying on God to bring him out of culture shock. He doesn't just read about God's faithfulness in the

Bible, or nod his head when people talk about it. He has lived it. He also learned that in times of pain and suffering he can find encouragement in God's Word. He knows as well that he can lean on his family and the Body of Christ, and that his brothers and sisters will walk beside him, pray for him, and not abandon him. He learned that sometimes our moments of greatest spiritual growth come when we are experiencing tremendous pain. Stretching and growing hurt!

When you are taken to the end of yourself and God becomes your only certainty, it deepens your relationship with Him. That is when you have to trust Him in ways you don't even imagine prior to reaching that point. What an amazing lesson to learn as a teenager. It would be one that God would use to mold Jordan into the man He created him to be.

Chapter 11

THE REAL HEROES

Gaining Perspective on Living by Faith

People who hear about my family's move to Southeast Asia often refer to it as a radical decision. That bothered all of us, because we didn't set out to do anything radical. We were simply doing what God told us to do. We had not given up anything of any real value, and we had been given so much in return. Besides, there is nothing radical about obedience. It's what all followers of Jesus are called to.

As a parent, when you tell your children to do something and they comply, do you consider them to be heroes just because they were obedient? I hope not! That is how we viewed our situation. God told us to do something, so we did it. Christians choose obedience over disobedience all the time, so we weren't doing anything remarkable. And frankly, given that 5,000 other Christians had answered Jesus's call to live and work overseas at the same time we were, it's clear that what we were doing wasn't extraordinary. We were obedient, but not heroic.

I'll never forget the first time we gathered with our co-workers for prayer after arriving in our new city. We were surrounded by the other

Americans who were working on our team in the same town, but there also were several Southeast Asian people present. Because it was our first week on the ground, we had not yet had any language training so I couldn't communicate with most of them.

I assumed, because this was a strict Muslim province, that these were local people who had wanted to gather with us to pray. I wondered if any of them were Muslim-background believers. No one offered an explanation, and my Western sensibilities told me it wouldn't be polite to ask. One of the young women greeted me in English, and I realized she had enough of a command of the language for us to hold a simple conversation.

I asked if she was a Christian and, as she shared her testimony, I learned that I was completely wrong about who was gathered in that room. I was surrounded by Christians who, just like my family, had been called by God to serve Him in this place! Glancing around, I counted at least fifteen Southeast Asian faces. God had called just as many of His children from within this country to serve Him in this city as he had called from America! What an incredible picture of God's plans and how I, or any other American, really isn't essential to getting His work done. After all, He was making a lot of progress before we even got started.

I knew that my national brothers and sisters in Christ had much better inroads to this culture than I ever could. I had so many barriers to overcome. I was a white, Western woman. And in most parts of the world, Christianity is seen as a white, Western religion. Thanks to American entertainment media, most of the world thinks of Western women as being immodest and promiscuous. That fuels another misunderstanding: if white, Western women are immodest and promiscuous, and white Westerners are Christian, guess what most of the world thinks about white, Western, "Christian" women? I was facing an uphill battle.

∞

In the part of the world where we were living, being a Muslim was part of a person's cultural legacy and identity. Having been raised in the Catholic church, I could understand what a cultural stronghold this was. I remember the struggles I had in the beginning to let go of the Catholic identity that had been drilled into me. It takes a long time, even when you are remaining within the Christian tradition.

I too had wrestled with the feeling that I had disappointed one of my parents. After all, being a Catholic was who and what I was raised to be. It wasn't until I began reading the Bible for myself and learning about Jesus that I was able to let go of my Catholic religion. I knew God could use my personal experience of letting go of traditions to embrace an eternal *relationship* with Jesus to reach Muslims who had a similar experience with generations of religious tradition.

I also knew that Muslims place a high value on modesty. So in order to be culturally appropriate, any time Molly and I left the house, despite the oppressive heat, we wore long-sleeved shirts and long pants or a long skirt. Also, because a head covering was a sign of modesty and the law for Muslim women, we chose to cover our heads as well. This was one way we could show our respect for the culture.

Although our manner of dress could be physically uncomfortable at times, it was appreciated by our local friends. We got a lot of "thumbs ups" for wearing a head scarf. It's a good thing we did, or we may have been tempted to not wear one, because it was really hot. Also, trying to understand a new language when your ears are covered presents its own challenges. Wearing the head scarf was a bridge to building relationships, but it also had a downside. Some people wrongly assumed we were Muslim.

Every time I felt hot or uncomfortable or unattractive, I reminded myself that our being called to this place had nothing to do with our personal comfort. And I knew how unimportant personal comfort was in comparison to the eternal destiny of the people we were living among. Besides, wearing the head scarf opened the door for some great conversations. Over time, it began to look strange and even offensive to me when I saw other Western women go out in public without one.

When people would see me, a white, Western woman wearing a head scarf, they almost always asked, "Are you a Muslim?" I would always respond, "No ma'am/sir, I am a follower of Jesus."

It was important to answer "follower of Jesus" rather than "Christian," because of the incorrect ideas they had about what being a Christian meant. For example, the locals thought Madonna the singer was a "really big Christian" because "she wears a really big cross." I needed them to understand that wearing a cross does not make you a Christian. They also assumed that all white Americans are Christians. They thought the Hollywood movies they had seen were a reflection of how Christians live.

The second question they would ask was why I was wearing a head scarf. I always responded, "Because I respect your culture." They would respond with "oh, thank you very much. You look beautiful in your head scarf." (Yeah right!)

Still, I knew I would never be able to get past the fact that I was a Western woman living in a Muslim culture. I decided that the best I could hope for was that in getting to know me, they would see a very different picture of a Christian woman. I wanted them to see a very clear picture of the Gospel in my family and the way we loved each other and the way we wanted to love them. But we also knew that Muslims would best come to know Christ through people who looked like them, spoke like them, and were part of their culture.

The national believers were living and working in our area at great personal risk. They could be beaten, tortured, and even killed just for sharing their faith. If the Western workers were caught doing the same thing, the penalty would be extremely mild by comparison. We might be asked to leave that area, and possibly the country, and not return.

∞

The Christian nationals had moved to this city to do community development work with Christians among the Muslim population, knowing that it could come at great personal cost. I can't think of a comparable situation for an American. I suppose it would be like asking a white, upper-middle-class person to move into the most crime-ridden ghetto and raise your children there. Would you be willing to do that if God asked you to? Probably not. And why? Because it isn't considered "safe" or "responsible."

But these national believers were putting their lives on the line to serve people, many of whom had lost everything in the tsunami. They had wholeheartedly responded to God's call to obedience.

The danger went beyond religious differences. The nationals had moved into an area of their country where a long-standing animosity existed between their people groups and the population of the city. The locals were seen by the rest of the country as "fanatics," and as a result, they viewed most other people groups in the country as not really being serious about Islam. They also felt that others had taken what was rightfully theirs in a province rich with natural resources. At times, the tension was thick. And yet these believers chose to come anyway, and for very little pay. Some were married and moved with their young children. Some were single women living in an area where a woman without a nearby husband or father can be the target of unwanted attention. They had planted themselves in a place where they could lose their life because of ethnic tensions and religious differences. All because they valued obedience to God and the absolute worth of the gospel above all other things.

Compared to these Christians, I hadn't risked anything. I was not likely to face real persecution. If you want to think about "radical obedience," think about the national Christians who were laying their lives on the line to serve God. I learned right away that they would need our most fervent prayers. Standing next to them, I felt ashamed that anyone would consider that my family had sacrificed anything to serve the Lord.

On another day I met my first Muslim-background believer. Here was living, breathing evidence that God will have people from "every tribe, tongue and nation" worship Him. This was happening here, in spite of Satan's attacks and the hardness of people's hearts.

I asked the man how he had become a believer. He said, "I studied Islam in college, and I wanted to disprove Christianity so I started to read the Bible. When I read Jesus's words, "I am the way, the Truth and the life. No one comes to the Father except through me" (John 14:6), I realized that Mohammed never said anything like that. I knew I had found the Truth."

It was that simple? Just one man, the Word of God, and the Holy Spirit? No Christian from the West armed with specialized strategies for sharing with Muslims and a library of books on Islam?

I love how God spoke directly to this man in such a simple and yet personal and profound way. He reminded me that it was just between him and God, and that it happened through his reading God's Word. I knew I did have a part to play in developing relationships with Muslims that would lead to sharing Truth, but that God didn't "need" me to get Muslims to believe. It was all His work. I was just privileged to play any part at all.

My brother in Christ went on to tell me that after he became a believer, his family rejected him. "But that's OK," he continued, "because I have all of you. When we are in the Body of Christ, we are all family."

That was a pretty amazing statement to make in a culture where family is everything. He had chosen to spend his life teaching others about Jesus. He wanted everyone to learn what he had learned about the truth of God.

This man has suffered intense persecution. He showed me scars where he had been severely beaten. He also had been arrested and tortured while in prison. His life has been threatened on numerous occasions, which forced him into hiding. As the Muslim community became aware that this man was following Jesus, an announcement was made on the local radio station that should anyone find him, they were to cut off his head. At that point, he decided to leave the area until things calmed down.

After my friend married, he and his wife had just one child, a son, whom the father was training, in his words, "to take my place after I die." Sadly that day would never come. His son was murdered when he became an adult. And just three days after his son was killed, this brother in Christ lost his wife.

I wondered how much one man can take. Now in his fifties, he is unable to get a job because of his beliefs. He said he spends his days "going out looking for people who need a place to stay. I invite them into my home and tell them stories about the prophets. When someone seems interested, I tell them about Jesus."

At the time I spoke to him, he had seen more than seventy-five people come to faith in Christ through his ministry. I knew I was looking in the eyes of not just someone who was risking everything, but someone who would likely be martyred. Humbled to be in his presence, I felt so small. I remembered all the times I had felt reluctant to share my faith back in the States because I might turn someone off or, even more embarrassing, the person might think I was weird and they wouldn't want to be my friend.

It was clear that I had much more growing to do.

Chapter 12

NEEDING EACH OTHER

Experiencing Christian Community in the Muslim World

One of the most surprising gifts we received came through the intimate relationships we developed with teammates. We served on a team with about eleven other Americans, some who had grown up overseas and others who, like us, were doing this for the first time. We learned a lot about being interdependent. We were a small minority group living in a strict Muslim area, and we realized immediately that we desperately needed one another.

Never having served in the military, I'm just guessing that our experience was similar to a Band of Brothers kind of fellowship. We really did have one another's backs. We had a shared vision and would do anything for one another. Living and working where we were, where the stress was high and the culture and the spiritual darkness overwhelming, we had to be intentional about being family to one another.

And that did something wonderful for our relationships, something that we don't see often in the West, where we value independence over community. We knew that we desperately needed one another, something that most Americans insulate themselves from. Americans place a tremendous value on individualism, which makes doing community very difficult.

Our Southeast Asia team shared a tremendous bond and commitment to one another. Our hearts, minds, and lives were yoked. We were family and, even better, we were the church in a place where there was no church...yet.

The closeness of our fellowship and the interdependence we experienced brought to mind a description of the early church: "And they devoted themselves to the apostles' teaching and the fellowship, to the breaking of bread and the prayers" (Acts 2:42).

We not only worked very hard as a team, we prayed together regularly and fervently. We studied the Bible together. We worshipped together. We celebrated together and cried together. We ate together regularly. Many on our team played Ultimate Frisbee on Sunday afternoons, and at other times we shopped, watched movies, played games, and just enjoyed being together. By leaning on the Body of Christ, we experienced what it means to live in real, authentic, biblical community. We saw how praying together and serving together, and choosing to love each other like family, is an amazing picture of one of the reasons God gave us the church.

Though we came from different backgrounds and were of different ages, there was no competitiveness like we often see in the States. We were equals in everything. It was refreshing and freeing.

Another community killer in American culture is our sense that being busy somehow proves that we are significant. Consider what not being busy might say about us: "I must not have any real purpose to my lie, since it's not slam-packed with activities and appointments. I'm not needed, thus I'm not significant."

But when we are busy, we don't have time to invest in community. In the gospels, Martha was busy while her sister, Mary, knew enough to take advantage of the opportunity to be with Jesus.

> Martha...had a sister called Mary, who sat at the Lord's feet, and listened to his [Jesus's] teaching. But Martha was distracted with much serving. And she went up to him and said, "Lord do you not care that my sister has left me to serve alone? Tell her then to help me." But the Lord answered her, "Martha, Martha, you are anxious and troubled about many things, but one thing is necessary. Mary has chosen the good portion, which will not be taken away from her." (Luke 10:38–42)

None of us have chance relationships. A relationship requires intentionality. Busyness has the effect of crowding out relationships. And when you are serving in a culture that is unlike everything you are accustomed to, you need the support of a community of believers.

The Western obsession with image and success—through busyness and being productive—is evident to outsiders. We asked our Muslim language tutor Glen what his honest impression of Westerners was. He was reluctant to respond, but after some encouragement he sheepishly replied, "You are always in a hurry."

Ugh. I started to watch some of the Westerners around town, mostly NGO workers who were there on a temporary assignment. The chief concern of many appeared to be to just fulfill their contract. I watched Westerners in airports, malls, and other areas throughout the country, and I realized that Glen was right. Americans move and behave as if we are in a hurry. So I resolved to purposely spend time with people, invest in them, and to make it clear that I did have time for them. When we intentionally spend time with someone, we let them know they really do matter.

I practiced this in Southeast Asia, among Muslim friends and also my teammates. In America we are so distracted and busy that we have little time or energy left for Christian community. But overseas, I had to depend on other believers. And whenever I wanted to do something with a teammate, I don't think I ever heard "I'm busy." The times I did hear it—or actually, read it—was in emails from friends back home.

I did not grow up in a family that encouraged, nurtured, or valued close relationships. When I was a child I did not know my extended family. My parents are divorced and my husband's mother passed away just two months after we were married, so our children have grown up without strong connections to extended family. But when we moved to Southeast Asia, my children gained a large, multi-generational family.

Workers with our overseas organization are called "aunts" and "uncles" by the children of the employees, because kids who grow up overseas miss out on typical extended-family relationships. For the first time in their lives, my children felt like they had aunts, uncles, and cousins. They felt truly known by adults other than their parents.

Our daughter, Molly, spent her middle-school years in Southeast Asia. She was not surrounded by other "tweens," but by godly men and women in their twenties, thirties, and forties. I joke with her that she is going to be the healthiest woman in America for having spent those important years surrounded by spiritually mature people who poured into her life and discipled her.

The same was true for Jordan, who spent his high school years surrounded by spiritually mature men and women. God not only met our needs but exceeded our expectations. Never before had I experienced the Body of Christ like I did when we lived in Southeast Asia. Never before had I felt such an interconnectedness with people. It was true biblical community.

Chapter 13

No Longer in Control

Overcoming the Lie That We Are in Charge of Anything

Throughout our marriage, I have often heard Curt say that the idea of control is an illusion. Yet Western culture sells us on the idea that we do control our lives, and human nature wants to believe it's true.

When we arrived in Southeast Asia we spent the first four weeks sleeping in bunk beds in a guest house, because the house that had been rented for us was being remodeled. We soon learned that in that part of the world, things don't get done or move quite as quickly as they do in the States.

But it wasn't just a matter of delayed remodeling. The house's owner had decided that renting to Westerners was an opportunity to charge high rent and use the money to renovate the house, which he would eventually live in. A contract was negotiated and a price determined long before we arrived. At that time, rental prices were much higher for Westerners who arrived to work in the area following the tsunami.

The homeowner set about making the house bigger and plusher

than anyone on our team had imagined. Meanwhile, he neglected to take care of some basic requirements. For example, staircases are notoriously steep in that part of the world, and while he was upgrading the house he failed to install a handrail up to the second floor. Neither did he add a knee wall at the front of the second-story balcony.

"That wasn't in the contract," was the owner's response. "If you want the railings and balcony wall, I'll need another $2,000. I've run out of money."

Considering the likelihood of earthquakes, we felt the railing on the steep staircase was pretty essential. We noted that the owner's addition of an extra room upstairs, a car port, and elaborate tile work wasn't in the contract, either. So how about a hand rail? This was the first of many lessons that made it clear we had no control over a life that we had come to believe was ours. Before we moved overseas, I had believed we could work, buy, and assemble our life into the perfect existence for our family. I remember slipping into "if only-ness," when Curt and I would convince ourselves that "if we could only" acquire this one thing, then we'd be all set.

But now, being immersed in a vastly different culture, the cycle of living in "if only" mode was over. We realized that thinking we could control life by assembling it just the way we wanted was controlling us.

We started to see the truth of this when Curt returned from his initial trip to Southeast Asia. He tried to put everything back into place at work, but his life as an IT director just didn't fit anymore. That was scary. How could the life we'd worked so hard for no longer fit us? God couldn't possibly want us to deconstruct everything we had put together over all these years and move to the Third World, right? Now, we have to laugh at God's sense of humor. He delivered us to a place and a culture that was so blatantly *out* of our control. We couldn't even pretend to control anything. The blatant contradictions and corruption was maddening at first. It grated against our self-righteous sense of "fairness." Adding to the reality of not being in control was the fact that when we first arrived, none of us had any useful skill with the language.

∞

When the home renovations were finally complete in the owner's eyes, we moved into the lovely yet imperfect house. We encountered a wealth of contradictions when dealing with the owner, who could be generous and gracious in his dealings with us. At the same time, he would be looking for new ways to take advantage of us.

Just about everything about our life on the island required more effort than it did back in the States. Things that required no thought or conscious effort at home now required intense concentration. When was the last time you had to bear down and focus while having a simple conversation? While driving? While shopping? When you live in a different culture, where English is not spoken, you have to be engrossed in every detail or you'll make a mistake.

It wasn't just issues with our house that turned our false sense of control upside-down. One afternoon, after the four of us had completed three hours of language training, we piled into the truck we were using to drive five miles to visit friends living at the guest house. When you are adjusting to a culture where you drive on the opposite side of the road, the steering wheel is on the opposite side of the vehicle, and there are no traffic rules, a million things race through your mind:

- OK, stay on the left side
- Watch out for motorbikes
- Remember, it's left on red
- Third gear is up and to the right, not left and...

As we pulled into the parking area we began to relax. We were back at our first home, a place where we felt at ease. Thinking it would make things easier when we were ready to leave, Curt backed the truck into a parking space. Glancing to his right, he maneuvered the truck to line up with a vehicle parked beside us.

CRASH!

There was a large mango tree behind us. The impact of the collision dented the tailgate and smashed the window of the cab.

In more than twenty years, Curt had not received a traffic ticket, much less been involved in an accident. He has one of the most steady, calm demeanors I have ever seen. But at this point he lost it. He jumped out of the truck to see the havoc he'd wrought and started shouting, "No! No! No!"

It was the first time I'd seen him lose it. He was furious with himself.

"Why does everything have to be so hard?" he asked.

Living half-way around the world, he had no control even over driving, something he had done without incident for more than two decades.

Later that afternoon he calmed down enough to go out again, this time with a friend to look at appliances for the house. The accident was still in the back of his mind and it was clouding his other thoughts. On top of that we were frustrated that we had just sold all the same appliances back in the States. Now we would be purchasing them again, but in a different country, using a different language, in a different currency, with unfamiliar brands to choose from. Curt began simmering all over again. As he tried to follow a conversation between our friend and a shopkeeper, he realized they were no longer talking about capacity and cost. Our friend, who had done business at this store before the tsunami, was inquiring about the storekeeper's son. The storekeeper's eyes turned red and tears welled up. On the morning of the disaster, the storekeeper and his son, who was Curt's age, were working together. After the earthquake, they began to set things right in the store. And that is when the first wall of seawater hit. As the two men scrambled to reach higher ground, the storekeeper watched as his son was carried away by the raging waters.

Suddenly the store got very quiet. The storekeeper turned and motioned toward refrigerators lined up along barren gray walls. "This was such a nice store before," he said.

∞

Curt told me the story. And later, as we rode home, we felt ashamed. Yes, our new life would be inconvenient and, sometimes, challenging. However, the frustrations with the house and the damage we caused to the truck we were driving would eventually become funny stories to share. But for the people living in this city, the loss of loved ones on the morning of December 26, 2004, would never become just a story to tell. We faced inconvenience, frustration, and irritations. But our neighbors had to live with deep-seated anguish.

Just a few hours after feeling angry over backing into a mango tree and feeling sorry for ourselves over our loss of control, we had a new perspective. There is no balm of this earth, no salve made by man, that could heal the pain that was there. And the control that we so longed to have, that we craved and deceived ourselves into thinking we had, turned out to be a trap.

Chapter 14

GOOD COMMUNITY DEVELOPMENT

Deciding How to Help

Before our arrival, the on-site team was engaged 24/7 in disaster relief. They focused on meeting the urgent needs of the community: body removal, providing clean water and adequate medical care, and putting a roof over people's heads, just to name a few. The scale was immense, but in time the work had to transition from relief to redevelopment. At that point the emphasis turned to restoring an infrastructure so that a devastated community could rebuild and then sustain itself.

With so many organizations working in the same place, often jockeying for position, we witnessed examples of good and poor community development. Large amounts of funding were flowing in, and grand ideas and promises were tossed around without careful planning or a definite commitment to follow through. This provided a fertile environment for miscommunication, frustration, and corruption.

In a rush to get started, many organizations began building houses before determining who would live in them. I have to believe that some structures were put up so the NGO could record the work in photos and videos, and use the visuals as a tool for fundraising. Many of these homes were built in previously uninhabited areas, were poorly constructed, and, in many cases, had to be torn down within a year because they were falling apart. Curt spoke with a director from a major global-relief organization about two years after the tsunami. He was told that the number of newly built houses scheduled for demolition would exceed the number they would be constructing.

In some instances, certain tsunami survivors were given multiple houses while others didn't receive even one. In other situations, people living outside the province at the time of the tsunami moved in afterward, taking homes away from families that had lived there for generations.

Our small organization was determined to avoid such pitfalls. We chose the area we would focus on, identified the community leaders, and began the slow but necessary process of establishing relationships. We were convinced that the healthiest form of community redevelopment is that which is done *with* the community rather than to or for the community. We were careful to work with community leaders to understand what the needs were.

In one sense, the people needed everything. However, it wasn't that simple. When rebuilding houses, we asked community leaders to determine which families' homes needed to be rebuilt, where they would be located, and in what order the houses should be constructed. We also needed to define in advance the process by which houses would be turned over to their new owners and the contributions that the community itself would make to their construction. Before a single foundation was dug, we worked alongside the community to define their needs and how they would be met, and set realistic expectations as to what would be done, when, and how.

While misunderstandings, broken promises, and shoddy construction forced several organizations to be run out of villages by angry residents, our organization kept its reputation intact, delivered on what was promised, and built solid relationships that continue to this day. And while most of our organization's projects could be considered successes, it is not surprising that what is most vivid in our memory are instances in which we saw a need but couldn't do more to help. One situation in particular still challenges Curt.

About two years after the disaster, a volunteer team of American doctors and nurses working with our organization provided a temporary clinic in a village that had been wiped out. The remaining villagers were housed in temporary barracks, hastily constructed by the government immediately following the disaster. During the clinic, a volunteer noticed that nearly all the people living in the barracks had holes in their clothes – even in the reasonably new clothes that had been donated. The volunteer asked why that was.

Through a translator, the volunteer learned that the barracks area was infested with large, bold rats. At night, rats would raid the barracks and chew through anything they could find. In the claustrophobic confines of the barracks, no one had anywhere to store their clothes and other possessions. The little they had was kept on the floor because there was no other choice. As a result, everything had holes. The villagers even told stories of rats nibbling on the feet of young children while they slept.

Our work in that area was limited to the timeframe of the temporary clinic. However, the concerned volunteer left us with a financial gift to be used to address the rat infestation. Exterminators don't work in that area, and rats are a relatively common fact of life in the tropics. Still, we came up with the best solution available. One week later, Curt returned to the village and helped distribute fifty plastic cabinets, fifty large rat traps, and fifty containers of rat glue. That supplied one set of materials for each household.

The families were grateful. The plastic cabinets would keep their possessions safe from rats, and the traps and glue would help reduce the vermin population.

Curt was thanked over and over for the fact that we had returned to help. One woman tugged at his arm and asked if we would return again to begin other projects in the area. Recognizing that budget restrictions and other planned work limited our ability to return, Curt reluctantly said that it wasn't possible. He told me later that he desperately wanted to say "yes," but he knew it would be impossible to live up to such a promise. Despite his response, the woman smiled, thanked him again, and walked back to the barracks.

Later that night, Curt said he had trouble sleeping. He kept wondering what was going on in the barracks. While he lay in the comfort of our bed with the gentle hum of air conditioning in the background, his thoughts returned to the people. No doubt, the stillness of the night was punctuated with the sounds of coughing, rats squealing, and traps slamming shut. He couldn't get these images out of his mind.

He admitted that a selfish part of him wanted to feel good about what we had done for the people. But he felt that he hadn't done anything. He felt even worse that he had been made aware of their plight and all he had done to help was to hand out storage containers and traps. And yet, for that, he received some of the warmest and most heartfelt expressions of gratitude ever.

The needs were overwhelming. In the case of this village, some of the residents may never know life outside of the barracks.

There is no mistaking the brokenness of our world. We couldn't help but reflect on the myriad of holes we were seeing...holes in clothes, holes in families, and holes in the hearts of the people. It was going to take so much more than new homes and new skills to rebuild this community.

Chapter 15

A DIFFERENT WAY
OF DOING THINGS

Finding That Most of Your Expectations Are 180 Degrees Off

You have probably read movie reviews that told you more about the reviewer than about the movie and its merits. A similar thing takes place when you start living in a culture that shares very little in common with your familiar milieu. Living in a new culture gives you a chance to see your background and customs through new eyes.

Have you ever been around kids when they play "opposite day?" When they say "yes" they mean "no," and vice-versa. The game never lasts long because it quickly becomes frustrating—even for the instigator. That's the way it sometimes felt to live in Southeast Asia. There were aspects of the cultural norms that were contradictory to Western practices. An early example was the issue of fairness. Living overseas gave me a new appreciation for how one-sided (and self-defined) our concept of fairness really is.

For example, soon after we settled into our rented house, Curt and

I were invited to appear on a radio station's English Corner program. As we drove to the studio, we felt a jolt from behind. A glance in the mirror told us everything. A speeding motorbike had skidded into our rear bumper. He had noticed too late that we were slowing down and signaling to turn right, and he was planning to pass us on the right.

The accident was his fault, but the local person who was riding with us encouraged us to keep going since the person on the motorbike was not injured. There are no laws against leaving the scene of an accident. And as long as the other party is not hurt, it's culturally acceptable to just drive off.

Still, the motorbike rider followed us to the radio station, where a discussion ensued. He wanted us to pay for the damage to his motorbike. But wait! We were slowing down and signaling to make a turn. That's when this man, on a speeding motorbike, hit our bumper, scratching it. And *we* are supposed to pay for damage to his bike, when it was clearly not our fault?

In this culture, no matter who is at fault, the driver of the larger vehicle is expected to pay for any damage to a smaller vehicle. (Insurance doesn't exist and the notoriously corrupt police, who usually demand a pay-off, are not helpful in settling a dispute.) We finally negotiated it down to terms that would have us pay half of what a reputable mechanic would charge for the repair. However, when the radio station owner learned of our plight, he stepped in to take care of the settlement. The motorcycle driver, realizing he wouldn't be able to squeeze money out of a local, drove off.

Later that week, we learned of a young university student who had been writing theses for several friends so that they could pass classes. When someone on our team mentioned that it wasn't right to do another student's work, she didn't understand. It wouldn't have been right to turn down a request for help, she explained. She was simply being a good friend by helping.

A short while later, we learned that a national friend of ours had found young hoodlums hanging out on his land, engaging in illegal activity. (Possession of narcotics can result in a death sentence, even though this province is known for its marijuana crops.) The land-owner attempted to run off the hoodlums, but they just laughed. Then he realized that one of the young men was the son of an influential religious leader in the area. He went to the holy man in private and asked him to intercede. Instead of helping, the holy man threatened to burn our friend's home and have him roughed up if he ever spoke of such things again.

The contradictions were thick and the standard of fairness was often the opposite of what I expected. Anger, self-righteousness, and irritation can bubble just below the surface if you let things such as this get to you. But, as He so often does, God always provided a way of bringing us back into the right focus. Living in a culture where it feels like there is no fairness brings you face-to-face with the reality that we are not there to judge another culture. My quest for fairness was mis-directed and, ultimately, self-defeating. I realized that if I got what I really deserved, I would be without any hope at all. Complete fairness would work against all of us.

∞

Life in Southeast Asia seemed at times like one constant adjustment, from the familiar to the foreign and back again. Some cultural differ-ences are charming, some are easily dismissed, and some require a for-eigner to take a deep breath and count to ten. But adjusting to cultural differences and embracing your new home has another side, and that is a matter of letting go of things you valued from your home culture.

I have mentioned that Curt and I willingly sold our house, our cars, and most of our possessions to respond to God's call. I didn't regret any of that. But a home represents much more than a mere possession. It stands for a way of life that you have grown familiar with. And in familiarity there is ease and convenience. You don't have to debate the propriety of waving at a neighbor, shopping in a store, or paying your bills every month. But when you live overseas, you find that ordinary actions, when done in public, carry unexpected baggage.

As it was, I found myself missing my home. We went from living in a brand-new home, and my enjoying a part-time job at my daughter's school, and having my own car to…living in a rented house that had no dishwasher or clothes dryer. It was full of cockroaches, ants, and geckos, and came equipped with uncomfortable furniture. The climate was incredibly hot, and I mean *incredibly*. Every day was like the hottest day in August in the hottest summer you can imagine, all year long. And I certainly couldn't dress in summer clothing.

Sometimes we had electricity and sometimes we didn't, for hours, even days at a time. Sometimes we had running water and sometimes we didn't. Our clothes had to be dried outdoors on a line, so our towels felt crunchy, bugs ate holes in our clothes, the colors faded, and everything felt stretched out. Because of the climate, I was sweating all day long, every day.

And climate aside, since we were living in a strict Muslim culture, every time I left my house I had to be sure I had on long sleeves, long pants, and a head covering. I didn't drive by choice because the absence of traffic rules intimidated me, so every time I wanted to go anywhere I had to get a ride from Curt. He never complained about it, but to me it was a loss of freedom.

I also went from cooking and cleaning my own home to having help come in. That may sound pretty great to you, and there are aspects that are indeed great, but it was hard too. I had lost another big part of our family routine. For the first time in my married life I didn't drive, I didn't clean, I didn't cook very much, and ninety-nine percent of the time I felt unattractive because of the clothing requirements for women, and because I was sweating constantly.

If all that weren't enough, occasionally I felt unwelcome just because of who I was. Here is a common conversation I would have in public. "Where are you from, miss?" "I am from the United States of America." (If we just said, "America," some would assume we meant South America.) "Ohhh America…George Bush…superpower…very bad," was one local man's response. On another day, while answering the same question, a man grew irritated and let me know in a loud voice, "I hate your president!" Interestingly enough, when Barack Obama became president during our time in Southeast Asia, the reaction changed. "Ohhhh Obama! Very good! Muslim!" was a frequent response.

∞

For six months we studied the national language with local tutors for four hours every day. It was exciting, boring, exhausting, and frustrating. The approach shared little in common with learning a language in high school or college. This time we were *immersed.* The sounds and intonations of the language were completely different from English, and at first it was hard to train our mouth and tongue to make sounds they'd never made before. Language learning is a humbling experience. You have to be willing to make mistakes, and a lot of them, and to acknowledge that you sound terrible. Then you keep trying while maintaining your sense of humor.

Our tutors were native speakers from our province, college students who also were proficient in English. In fact, English was their *third* language, as they spoke not just the national language but a local dialect as well. Some of them were also fluent in Arabic, the language of the Al Qur'an, and some were studying French and Mandarin. It was a little embarrassing to be so much older than they were, hailing from a First World country, and able to speak only one language.

During each hour of instruction we took a break, which gave us a chance to talk to our tutors on a more personal level. We asked questions about their culture, their lives, and their beliefs. We asked one tutor if he had ever seen a white person before the tsunami brought in so many foreign relief workers. He said he had a few times at the beaches, which attract foreign surfers, but the people he had seen were usually from Australia.

He said that before the Western relief workers arrived, locals used to always smile at everyone. But when so many white people arrived, people stopped doing that. We wondered why.

"Because," he said, "we didn't know if they [the white Westerners] would smile back. We didn't know what they were thinking."

I wondered how closely his observation was associated with an earlier observation that Westerners always seem to be in a hurry. In this Asian nation, people take time with each other. They are intentional and personable. There is no need to rush because their culture is not time-sensitive. This can be frustrating for a newly arrived Westerner, but after a while you realize that it can be a nice way to live!

There are no such things as appointments, because things are done relative to the five prayer times of the day. Muslims are obligated to pray at sunrise, around noon, in the late afternoon, at sunset, and in the late evening, so their days tend to revolve around those times, which vary according to the rising and setting of the sun and moon. You would never schedule an appointment around the noon or sunset prayers. If you wanted to meet someone after "lunchtime," you would gather sometime after the obligatory noon prayers. That meant the person would show up any time between one and three in the afternoon. We had no choice but to lay down our sensitivity to time.

One of our favorite activities was to frequent a juice bar. It was really just an open-air room, furnished with plastic tables and plastic chairs. A man stationed behind a cart made fresh-squeezed juice from fruit that the customer had selected. Once you patronize a local business and then return, you are greeted like a friend. One evening Curt introduced me to the proprietor of the juice bar. As we chatted, he invited us to sit and enjoy the beautiful evening weather. We probably sat there for twenty minutes while he made the juices. A quick juice run became a forty-minute event, but it included relaxation, the enjoyment of beautiful weather, and a nice visit with the juice maker.

Relationships really are important there. Whenever we entered a restaurant, a juice bar, or a store, we were honored as a guest. When we came back, then we were their friend. Eventually we would be invited into their home, after which we would be treated as a member of the family.

Even in casual encounters on the street I don't think we ever met a person who looked past us or who dismissed us with a quick hello as they passed by. Once we let go of our Western sense of time, we began to like the more relaxed pace of life. As soon as our language tutor confessed to us what he thought of white people, I became more intentional. I didn't want people to see me as just another hurried white person.

God meant for us to enjoy Him and to be in community with other people. God values relationship, so I wanted the locals to see that we had time for them. I would never be able to be an insider, but I wanted to be an acceptable outsider. I knew that I had to make some changes.

∞

For me, most of the hardest adjustments had to do with a loss of personal comfort. It helps to remember that when Jesus invites us to follow him, he doesn't say "Come, follow me and be comfortable." Jesus calls us to obedience, which is sometimes anything but comfortable.

However, obedience is not complicated. Jesus calls you to follow Him, and answering that call is simple and straightforward. What often gets in the way is our expectations. If you expect accolades, or an improved life, or popularity, or serenity, you'll be disappointed when those things don't materialize. But if you take Jesus's call at face value, you can view shifts in your life in a different perspective.

I realized how unimportant personal comfort really is. I knew that God had called us to this Muslim province, and I knew that the One who called us is faithful. The fact that Jesus was there ahead of us, and had invited us to participate in the work He was already doing, was enough.

Although I did miss my friends back in the States, in our time in Southeast Asia the Lord gave us wonderful relationships. I realized there was nothing coincidental about the people we were meeting. The Lord is sovereign over all things at all times, so I understood that He had arranged my meetings with others. That changed my perspective on relationships, and it made it easier when I started missing my friends from the States.

Every person I met was someone the Lord orchestrated for me to meet. That is true whether you live in Asia or North America. Try to recognize other people not as interruptions, or as excessively needy, or a test of your patience, but as someone God put in your life. See if it makes a difference in the way you approach the people you meet.

∞

Since we were living in a strict Muslim province, we couldn't attend church. There was a Catholic and a Methodist church in our city, but they were primarily for the local Chinese population. We decided not to attend either church, not for ethnic or theological reasons, but because we wanted to model something different. We knew that a native would be arrested if he or she were seen attending a church service. For Chinese business owners it was acceptable. But for the local population it was in violation of Shari'a law.

So the team members gathered instead as a house church—a small group of believers coming together for worship, Bible study, and prayer. We also gathered weekly just for prayer, usually on Fridays at noon during the time that our Muslim neighbors were praying. That worked well until one week when we were gathered at our house, in an upstairs room. We began our time with singing, foolishly forgetting to close the windows. Leaders from the mosque next door banged on our door, angry that our singing had disturbed Friday prayers. We apologized and from that point on we met in a teammate's house.

In the States my family was active in the ministries of The Summit, a multi-site megachurch. Most of our closest relationships were with people from that church. We had decided that while we lived in Southeast Asia, we would try to listen to J.D. Greear's sermons via podcast, if we had electricity.

I missed our home church, and looking back to what I had lost colored my feelings about the small group that met as a house church. But we were living in a land where there was no institutional church available to Americans. So our small gathering, while new to all of us, was important.

After a few months, Curt and I decided that we needed to be intentional about building the community of our house church. So on Sundays we started gathering first for dinner, crowding around our dining-room table. We shared stories and the events of the week. Afterward, we moved to the living room and our son, Jordan, would play his guitar and lead us in worship. It was our group's preference that one of the husbands would lead our time of teaching. We generally would go through a study of a book of the Bible. We would have lively discussions, and then close with prayer and end our evening with dessert and hanging out.

It wasn't long before the sweetness of the intimacy of our gatherings became a high point of the week. This unfamiliar form of church became one of the highlights of our three years in Southeast Asia. We grew together in our sense of community, in our interconnectedness, and in our dependence on the Holy Spirit to teach us. Church, like celebrating Christmas in a strict Muslim province, became something we had to create, not consume. And that made it precious.

Chapter 16

WATCHING MY KIDS SOAR

A Mother's Concern for the Well-Being of Her Children

One of the things Curt and I wrestled with before we moved overseas was the impact such a move would have on our children. We didn't have toddlers who would grow up bicultural without even realizing it. We had a teenager and a tween, both of them very settled in our community, and both with interests and activities that were important to them. We assumed Jordan and Molly would have to let go of their particular extracurricular pursuits after we moved overseas.

We were wrong about that, but after we relocated we realized our kids had no peers to socialize with in our new city. They went from spending the majority of their day surrounded by kids their own age to the reality that the only other Americans in their world were at least ten years older than they were. The only other American kids were considerably younger, and the kids that were their age were Asian. They were cut off from peers by language and culture. Local teenagers would stare at Jordan and Molly, reacting to their presence by whispering and sometimes giggling. They would usually run away if my kids tried to engage them in conversation.

I couldn't help but ask myself, "Whaaat have we done?" The transition was hard enough on Curt and me, but it was far harder to watch my kids face so many changes. I wanted to make everything as smooth as possible for them. Now I started to question myself. Had I put them in a situation that wasn't fair to them?

I needed to face some facts and adjust my approach accordingly. First, I realized the worst thing I could do for my family was to compare where we were with our previous life. The second worst thing was to try to duplicate an American lifestyle in our new home. We all needed to see what life had in store for us in a new culture. We needed to expect something different, something that might not be worse than what we were used to.

I might have been worrying unnecessarily. Jordan and Molly welcomed the new experiences that came their way. They were naturally curious and engaging, which was key to their getting through culture shock and feeling at home in their new country.

They studied language, were intentional about meeting people, tried new foods, and joined in with cultural traditions and activities—even when it wasn't easy or comfortable. They got involved in the work our team was doing and made their own relationships with national believers. Our family shifted from living by four separate schedules in North Carolina to becoming a unified team, all having a likeminded focus, direction, and lifestyle.

One of the greatest gifts was the development of Jordan and Molly's already-close sibling relationship. They spent every day together, not just homeschooling but playing games, listening to music, and talking for hours. And beyond developing close relationships with members of our team, God gave each of them their own roles in our new city.

Jordan developed incredible social skills that made everyone he met feel comfortable and welcomed. He remembered details about conversations he had had previously with someone, so that the next time he saw the person he could ask how things were going—and mention specifics. His natural sweetness and friendly demeanor made him a real hit with the locals.

Although he was studying the national language with us every day, through relationships with locals he began to pick up the local dialect. To see a foreigner be able to converse fluently in the national language is impressive to Southeast Asians. But Jordan went a step beyond, learning the local dialect. Because of his natural ability to connect with people, Jordan was able to share the gospel numerous times with locals. I'll never forget the time he got in the car as we were leaving a friend's house. He was uncharacteristically very emotional and said, "I just said the hardest thing I have ever had to say. Usher [a Muslim friend] asked if I thought he was going to heaven when he died and I told him, 'No Usher, I know that you aren't.' That was really, really hard."

My teenage son felt the weight of his friend's lostness, and that had a huge impact on him. He continued to grow close to Usher and have deep spiritual conversations with him. It was amazing to see Usher, a man in his early thirties, have such deep admiration and respect for a young man half his age.

Jordan also got close to our team of national believers through volunteering at our organization's farm, which was used for agricultural training. After his first day at work, on what was an exceptionally hot day, he came home and said, "I loved it."

"What did you do?" I asked.

"We went into the mountains and got food for the goats. Then we walked on the beach and picked up cow poop to make fertilizer. It was awesome."

You know your son is passionate about his work when walking on a beach in 100-degree-plus temperatures picking up cow poop makes his heart sing. Jordan really enjoys working outdoors, and being on the farm provided some of his happiest experiences. It was through his volunteering there that he learned that he did not want to work a desk job in the future!

While my friends' kids dream of BMWs and six-figure incomes, my son has been thinking about how he might spend his life as a community developer.

vWe hadn't anticipated the full impact of our kids being surrounded by wise mentors overseas, but it turned out to be one of the greatest blessings in their lives. Between the ages of fifteen and eighteen, Jordan spent incredible amounts of time with spiritually mature, godly men. These talented men had left the comforts of life in the States to do what Jordan now wanted to do in adulthood. I couldn't have asked for a better internship for my son.

Jordan also discovered and developed a gift for leading worship. He had been a proficient trumpet player back in the States, but he brought a guitar with him overseas. He'd had a few lessons before leaving the States, but for the most part he taught himself to play by listening to CDs and figuring out the guitar parts. In a very short time he got so good that he was able to play by ear and lead worship.

The guitar brought him hours of entertainment and pleasure in a place that offered few options for an American teenager. It also gave him leadership opportunities as he chose the music for our house church and at a summer camp he attended. And best of all it gave him a connection with locals.

One day we were helping to teach English at a high school, and Jordan struck up a conversation with some of the students. When they found out he was a guitar player they asked him to come jam with their band. For a brief time Jordan fulfilled the dream of many high school boys when he became a guitar player in a band called Panic.

Like Jordan, Molly became close with the children of our coworkers, as well as the young adults we were serving with. A few of the women on our team spent intentional time with her. Like Jordan, her "peers" were a group of godly women in their mid-twenties to mid-thirties.

Molly served the young mothers on our team by caring for their babies and toddlers so they could have a night out or just take a badly needed break.

∞

I had promised Molly before we left the States that I would do whatever I could to help keep her ballet training going. At first that meant encouraging her to keep practicing on her own, in a house with only tile floors, in an incredibly hot climate. We used air conditioning only at night while we slept. Most girls her age would have quit. And although there were times when I am sure she felt it was futile, she didn't quit. We had brought a portable ballet barre with us to the other side of the world, and several times a week Molly would change into her leotard and tights, set up the barre, play a CD of ballet music, and get to work. She did that on a regular basis for three years.

There was no ballet in our strict Muslim province, but there was a form of local, traditional dance. We found a home in our neighborhood where traditional dance was taught on Saturday mornings. Molly began attending the practices, where none of the other girls would talk to her. But often they would stare, whisper, giggle, and point. The instruction was done in a language she couldn't yet understand, and the dance movements were unlike anything she had done or seen before. She picked it up quickly, and it wasn't long before she was as proficient as her peers. Although it was challenging to learn a completely new way to move her body, and it was fun to have such a rich cultural experience, it was no replacement for ballet.

A few months after we arrived in country, we attended a home-school conference with other American families living in Southeast Asia. I shared Molly's story about laying down her ballet dreams and the young mothers asked if Molly would teach their daughters ballet. Molly was thrilled to do this, and spent one afternoon sharing her gifts with about fifteen young girls.

One night as the attendees were gathered for a science fair, Molly was asked to perform. Dancing for a few moms and their daughters during her afternoon class was different than dancing for sixty people, not just moms, but also few dads who were in town for a meeting, plus teenagers. She's never been one for stage fright, but as the crowd began to chant her name her eyes welled up. I asked if she wanted me to get her out of it, but she agreed to perform and began putting on her pointe shoes.

As she did this, a small crowd of younger girls gathered around her, asking questions, watching her get ready. It was such a precious sight to see the younger girls admiring her. It reminded me of when she was a little girl herself, the way she would watch the older dancers, soaking in their every move. I could see her start to relax as she patiently and cheerfully explained to the younger girls how a ballet dancer ties the ribbons on her pointe shoes.

Before she began her performance, I explained to the audience how the hardest thing for Molly to give up wasn't her friends, her school, the food, or any of the other typical things back in America. It was ballet. I told them that what they were about to see was an awesome testimony of God's provision, protection, and faithfulness. Everything they were about to see, Molly had learned on her own, without the benefit of an instructor, but very much with the benefit of her Creator. When you lay something down for God's glory, He blesses it. Every time.

She performed the Marzipan Princess dance from The Nutcracker, which she had taught herself by watching a video. She was breathtaking. After the roaring applause, I think every person present came up to say how much they enjoyed her performance. Many adults had tears in their eyes. Other girls said, "You were awesome! You were so beautiful!"

Seventh grade girls actually said that. Think about when you were in seventh grade. How often did one girl give another girl such heartfelt praise in front of others? As much as I was moved and blessed by my daughter's performance, the biggest blessing was to witness other team members becoming our family. They supported, loved, and encouraged us in a way that I had never experienced before. The outpouring of love was something I will never forget.

Molly wasn't dancing for herself or for the audience. She was dancing for the One who had given her the gift of ballet. When she was willing to lay it down, God grew it, protected it, and blessed it. His work in her life was on display that night, and what a beautiful sight it was.

It was a huge turning point for my daughter. Through that one performance in a hotel in Southeast Asia she knew that God is able. He had not forgotten her. She could trust Him.

While her peers in America were getting themselves to class every day and following the instructions they were being given, Molly was learning how to dance from the inside out. How can you explain a young ballet student improving when she had no formal instruction for several formative years? It was not the work she put in upstairs in the makeshift dance studio in our home, but what God was doing in and through her that was making her dancing so spectacular.

∞

But like Jordan with culture shock, Molly had her struggles as well. When we moved overseas she was eleven, and when we came back home she was fourteen. She's petite, but during the years we lived overseas she was growing into a young woman. One of the hardest things we experienced was relentless male attention in public. Although she and I were always completely modest and covered, the leering and the comments could become unbearable. It made her brother incredibly protective of her, and that was a good thing for him to feel and for her to see.

Soon after we moved into our house, Molly was loaned a bicycle by one of the women on our team. She would ride it around and around a large field in front of our house. It was an activity that made her feel normal when everything else was so incredibly different. She loved that bike.

In America, a pretty girl riding a bicycle would draw little attention. But in our neighborhood, a couple of young boys began to harass Molly. They would call out to her, and she would ignore them. However, one day the ringleader, a ten-year old named Pokey, ran up and grabbed Molly's waist when she rode by. He and his cohorts than ran off laughing. The rest of us knew something bad had happened when Molly ran inside, out of breath and with tears in her eyes.

Curt and one of our teammates ran after the kids and they scattered, laughing and mocking Curt's attempts at yelling at them in their language. Jordan was livid.

A few weeks later, we were having lunch when we heard laughter coming from behind the house. The same kids were swimming in the river behind our house…minus their clothing. It's a cultural thing, so we didn't take action to stop it, even though we didn't care for it. But things took a turn for the worse when several of the boys climbed over a wall into our back yard and began grabbing papayas from our trees. They were making a mess. I stepped outside to ask them to leave. Most of the boys jumped back over the wall, but Pokey stood on the wall and began laughing hysterically. Then he went even further, gyrating his naked hips toward me.

Jordan was steaming by this time. Pokey had messed with his sister and now had insulted his mother. One ten-year old boy had decided to harass us. We told Jordan to turn the other cheek and try to understand the pain this kid had experienced. (We had learned that Pokey had lost his dad to diabetes just a year earlier.) However, Jordan's heart, normally the softest in our family, was hardened against this kid.

Then something changed. Several months after these incidents, our house helper and friend, Natalie, invited us to join her, her family, and her entire village for an afternoon at the beach. The Sunday before the fasting month of Ramadan begins is traditionally a day when locals gather for picnics at the beach. It's a festive atmosphere, similar to American get-togethers on the Fourth of July.

Since Pokey lived in Natalie's village, we assumed he would be at the beach. Natalie didn't own a car, so we stopped by to pick up her family. In our city there were no rules about the number of passengers you could have in one vehicle, probably because, among other things, seat belts were not required. When we arrived at her house, person after person filed into our van.

We were a little surprised when Pokey climbed in, and even more so when he placed himself in my lap! Jordan was subdued on the way to the beach, intently watching Pokey. Curt was quiet as he drove, wondering what kind of day we had gotten ourselves into.

Once at the beach, it seemed as if the entire population of the region had turned out. Thousands of locals were milling around. Techno music blasted from giant speakers, and people waded into the ocean (fully clothed, including head coverings for the ladies). Families grouped together with others from their village, and outside the four members of my family, not another white face was in sight.

Remarkably, we found an empty spot near others from the village and unloaded our stuff. Curt grabbed a Frisbee and got Jordan involved in a game of catch. To say that they attracted attention would be an understatement. You could feel the eyes on them as they played. Once the heat got to be too much, Jordan headed to the water's edge to cool off. Within a few minutes, we realized that Jordan was horsing around, laughing and splashing with a little kid. It was Pokey.

Huh?

Curt headed down to the water and caught Jordan's eye.

"You know Dad, If I had run into Pokey last week I don't know what I would've done. I loathed the kid. But now we're having the best time."

Despite his initial anger, by praying for Pokey, even when he didn't really feel like it at first, God had softened Jordan's heart. Off and on throughout the day, the two of them would wander off, chatting and laughing. At one point I smiled at Pokey, pointed at Jordan, and said, "He is like a big brother for you, huh?"

His eyes got wide and he smiled. Big brothers were a huge deal in our province. They were highly respected. In a matter of hours, God had broken down the obstacles of age difference, culture, ethnicity… and anger. On the beach, after having spent many weeks praying for Pokey, Jordan's heart was broken for this boy.

Molly, who had forgiven Pokey for squeezing her waist that day, was relieved to see Jordan's heart change. Although she was grateful for her brother's protective nature toward her, she did not want to see Jordan harden his heart toward the people we were living with. It would not have been culturally appropriate for Molly to join in on Jordan and Pokey playing together on the beach. Instead, Molly and I sat at a distance, surrounded by the other women, as we watched God transform a relationship that had impacted us all.

Chapter 17

BEAUTY FROM ASHES

Having Your Faith Stretched to the Limit

When you answer Jesus's call you are taking a step of faith. And while a life of obedience deepens your faith in ways you can't predict, it also puts you in situations that test it. During our years in Southeast Asia, Curt and I succeeded in accepting or at least abiding by many cultural values that ran counter to our own convictions. But following an accident that injured a good friend—and the compounded harm that was done to this woman because of long-held traditions and biases—life overseas came close to pushing me to the brink.

A woman with high intelligence and charm to spare, our friend Lee was part of a culture that devalued women, no matter how much talent and promise they showed. And beyond that, Lee's Islamic religion and traditions dictated that children must obey their parents' wishes. *Not* honoring one's parents is considered one of the biggest sins in Islam.

We learned about this ingrained behavior from Lee when she was tutoring us in the language. She has a magnetic personality that everyone is drawn to. She is so warm, smart, talkative, and fun to be with.

We first met when Lee was twenty-four. Although she was then a medical student, she had always dreamed of being an architect. But since no one from her village had ever become a doctor, her parents had decided that she would be the first. Her parents decreed that becoming a pediatrician would be her destiny, and her only option was to honor their wishes.

When I asked Lee where she found her motivation to pursue a career she had no passion for, she said, "I just think about the people in my village." What a jolt to my Western bias in favor of "be anything you want to be." In stark contrast, Lee would be "anything *her parents* wanted her to be."

She was about half-way through her medical training when we first met. She had just completed the classroom portion and was in the first year of an internship when she had a life-changing motorbike accident.

It was a Friday afternoon in April, and the noon prayers were over. Lee was on her way to her parents' village for a weekend visit, about three hours away, when she stopped on the side of the road to get some food. In this part of the world people rarely wear a helmet when riding a motorcycle. Lee took wearing a helmet a little more seriously. But, as was typical for a local, she didn't usually buckle it. That day after buying her food, Lee was getting back on her bike when a man she had never seen before told her to put her jacket on and buckle her helmet. It was advice that only minutes later would save her life.

As she continued on her journey, her motorbike was struck by a car, knocking Lee and her bike to the ground. In this part of the world, because of the abundance of motorbikes and the absence of traffic rules, accidents are common. In most cases, locals pick themselves and their motorbikes up and continue on their way. But Lee had been seriously injured, and the car that hit her never stopped.

There is no 911 service available. When accidents happen, you rely on the people around you to transport you to the hospital. Lee was in a rural area, some distance from what would be considered good medical care by local standards. A witness called a friend at the Red Cross, and Lee was taken to the "best" hospital in the province's capital city. This was just a few minutes' drive from where we were living.

We headed straight for the ER, where friends were gathered, keeping vigil as Lee lay on a table just inside the door. It wasn't long before her family arrived, and understandably they were very shaken. Lee's mother greeted everyone who had come in support of her daughter. We were considered honored guests.

∞

Early in the evening, and simply because I asked, I was invited to stand by Lee's bed in the ER. As I made my way from the waiting area to the ER's front door, I saw the familiar pile of shoes. In Asia, the custom is to remove your shoes before you enter a home, but in the *hospital*? Yes, even in the hospital.

With my shoes off, I was immediately struck by how dirty the floor felt. I cringed as I spotted mangy cats wandering in and out of the ER. Inside was a sea of beds, and everyone—patients, doctors and nurses—turned to stare at the white woman in a head covering.

I didn't see a single curtain to give any of the patients privacy, nor did I see one latex glove, surgical mask, sink, bar of soap, or bottle of hand sanitizer. It couldn't have been more different than uber-sterile, modern UNC Hospital where I had been with Jordan only ten months before.

God, give me grace and give me strength to face what I am seeing. I need it, I prayed.

Lee's swollen face made her nearly unrecognizable. Her head was in a brace and she was moaning nonstop. I could see a large bone in her leg protruding through the skin. It grieved me to see my dear friend so seriously injured, lying out in the open in what I perceived to be a very unsanitary ER.

No nurses were attending to her. No IVs had been administered, and no pain medication given. It was almost too much to bear.

I rejoined the friends who were seated on benches outside the ER, as people text messaged all over the city looking for blood donors. When a patient needed blood, it was up to friends and family to find donors. Nine people with A+ blood were needed and several were located, but many were rejected for low hemoglobin. So the frantic search resumed. As potential donors were found, Curt drove people to and from the blood bank, at a different location than the hospital. At 1 a.m. we headed home to get our kids into bed—without word on when our friend would go into surgery.

The following day we learned that Lee had been moved to another hospital in our city. The first hospital didn't have the needed instruments and a machine used to sterilize instruments was broken. She finally went into surgery twenty-five hours after her accident. Again, I had to let go of my cultural response to the situation. The doctor had informed the family that they could expect the surgery to last two hours. Curt and I arrived shortly before surgery began at 5 p.m..

We made our way up dangerously steep, unfinished, concrete stairs. There was no hand railing, and we noticed that the floor underneath our feet was dirt. Not dirty, but dirt. The waiting area outside the OR consisted of two benches, a dirt floor, concrete walls, and a partial tin roof. A large part of the room was open to the outdoors. If it had rained we would have been soaked. It looked more like a construction zone than an operating suite.

I asked Curt, "Are they tearing this place down due to earthquake damage, or are they building an extension?"

I was growing weary of what I was seeing. I badly wanted to help dear Lee, who seemed to be at great risk. She was about to undergo major surgery in an area with inadequate health care. I was so angry at the system, so shocked at the conditions that all of the locals so readily accepted, and so fearful for Lee's survival, let alone her future. I knew I needed to calm down. I reminded myself that what I was seeing was bothering me because I was an American and used to very different standards in healthcare. I tried to take my cues from the locals, who didn't seem bothered at all by the primitive surroundings.

Here is an example of how readily the locals accepted the conditions at the hospital. Leaning against a concrete wall I saw a row of tanks containing highly flammable oxygen. Next to the tanks were windows with no glass. A man was sitting in a window opening right next to the tanks smoking a cigarette.

We were told by a friend that earlier, hospital personnel had carried Lee on a stretcher up those same steep, concrete, railing-less stairs, and across the dirt floor into the operating room. Remember that Lee had a leg bone protruding through her skin, along with many other serious injuries, and she had been in severe pain for twenty-five hours. It was hard to understand how she could be treated so carelessly, even in a Third World country. It was wrong.

As the hours passed, friends and family gathered outside the OR, waiting for news. Two hours became six as we talked with friends late into the night. Lee was still in her two-hour surgery when we left around midnight. The doctor never came out to tell the family why surgery took so much longer than anticipated. You are simply expected to wait, not ask.

Every night for the next three nights we visited Lee in the hospital. Now that her eyes were open, we saw they were purple on the outside and red on the inside. There was a bandage on her lip, and she had lost some teeth. She also had a cast on her leg, a brace on her hip, abrasions on her face, and her mouth was so swollen she was unable to speak. All she could do was moan. It is expected that your family will care for you when you are in the hospital, so her relatives were essentially living in her hospital room, sleeping on rugs that they had brought from home. Lee lay on a bed with a frighteningly thin mattress, covered by a sarong that had been brought from home, with a single IV line dripping fluids into her arm. Even though she was running a fever, no antibiotics or pain medication was in the IV. When she felt pain, she was told "not to think about it."

By the fourth day she was alert and the swelling in her mouth had gone down enough that she was able to talk. When I asked what the doctor had said about her condition, I was surprised to hear that she hadn't yet seen a doctor, just a nurse. And the nurse had told her to hold any questions for a doctor. And this was seventy-two hours after Lee's surgery.

After several weeks, Lee was declared well enough to be released. She was on crutches and still unable to bend her knee, and as weeks and then months passed, it became apparent that she wasn't making progress. So I asked doctor friends in America to review her x-rays just to see if something had been missed, and, honestly, to help relieve my worries.

The news was not good. Although the American doctors were reluctant to criticize another physician's work, there was concern that the screw that had been inserted in her knee was not only the incorrect size, but it looked to have been put in the wrong place. I was advised to encourage Lee to get a second opinion. But with only one orthopedist practicing in the province, that was not an option. When I would ask Lee about her knee and what she thought about her progress, she would respond in the same way: "I think it's getting better. I just have to be patient." We learned that this was the only culturally acceptable response she could give.

It couldn't be true that she was getting better. It wasn't hard to see pain and worry underneath her cheerful exterior.

One night Lee brought a friend to our house to watch the movie "The Count of Monte Cristo" with us. There is a line of dialogue in the movie that stood out to me that night even though I had seen the movie many times: "You may have forgotten God, but he hasn't forgotten you…" I looked over at Lee and squeezed her hand. I knew that I needed to speak to her again about her health and the lack of progress with her leg.

That evening I casually asked how she was doing, how her leg was feeling. She ran my fingers over her knee and let me feel the screw inside, which was a hard metallic presence just under the surface of the skin. With a smile on her face that betrayed what was really going on inside, she put her two feet side by side and showed me how the foot on the injured leg was atrophying. Her toes were curling and she said that foot always felt cold.

Lee was hiding a lot of pain, both physical and emotional. I decided it was time to be more of a mom to her, so I convinced her to make an appointment with the orthopedic surgeon. This was to be her first appointment with him, almost five months after her accident.

On the evening of her appointment a teammate and I took Lee to the clinic. We could see how frightened she was, but I didn't understand why at the time. Before we got out of the car to walk to the office, I asked if I could pray for her. Though she was a Muslim and I am a Christian who prays in the name of Jesus, we had done this many times before. She agreed, and we bowed our heads. I asked God to make His presence known to Lee as she met with the surgeon, and to show her that she was not walking into it alone. I prayed for wisdom for the doctor to know exactly how to help her. I asked God to give the doctor a plan that would lead to the healing of Lee's still-injured leg. I then turned my attention to Lee and told her that God never promised us an easy life, but on behalf of her I was claiming His promise to never leave us and never forsake us.

We all said "Amen" and got out of the car.

Chapter 18

TRUSTING GOD TO OVER-COME EARTHLY POWER

Seeking Him Even When Every Visible Force Is Opposing You

It was around 9 p.m. when we walked into the clinic, as doctors in our province only had office hours in the evening following the Muslim sunset prayer time. We walked into a waiting room crowded with more than one hundred people. There was no receptionist to check in with, and no insurance information to supply because Lee, like most locals, didn't have any. All eyes were fixed on the two white women in head scarves walking in with a local girl on crutches.

We found a few available plastic chairs along the wall and sat down to wait. I tried to smile and be positive. I wanted to communicate encouragement and hope to Lee as I tried to ignore the rats running across the floor of the dirty waiting area. Amazingly, Lee's name was called rather quickly. She walked through the door, X-rays in hand from earlier that afternoon. My teammate and I waited and prayed. Five minutes later, her appointment was over. *Five minutes later.*

Again I had to fight back a sinking feeling. How could such a complicated injury and subsequent lack of recovery be adequately assessed in just five minutes? I needed to put my feelings aside and constantly remind myself that I was a guest in this culture. So I followed Lee's lead. She was surprisingly calm, composed, and even positive. Had I misread the situation, imposing my own Western cultural expectations and completely missed the mark? Once we got to the car I couldn't hold it in any longer.

"What did the doctor say?" I asked, hoping it was better than what I feared.

She reported that the doctor didn't look at her leg, but he did quickly glance at the X-ray. Then, while he wrote on a piece of paper, his only instruction was for her to go down to using just one crutch after the fasting month holiday. (That was six weeks away.) When Lee asked why he thought she still wasn't able to bend her knee, he said without looking up, "Because your fracture isn't being polite."

Whaaat?! If I ever came close to losing it while living overseas, that was the moment. I could have endangered our work there and given the Western workers a bad name if I had publicly expressed what I was feeling. It might even have caused my family to be welcomed out of the province. But I was so angry at the way the doctor had dismissed Lee and her suffering, and so disbelieving that he could be so cavalier with the performance of his profession, that I wanted to rush back into the clinic. I was prepared to tell the doctor what I thought of him, and to demand that he provide adequate care. But under the circumstances, I couldn't.

Instead, I remained in the car with Lee and continued to listen. She said she asked the doctor if she should continue her physical therapy, noting that she had not made any improvement since beginning it. And again, without looking up, the doctor said, "Well, you can…"

He told her that after the fasting-month holidays had passed, they could discuss the possibility of further surgery, though he said her chances of ever walking again, especially without crutches, were about 50/50. The customs of their culture prevented her from asking many questions or demanding answers. Doing so would make her appear to be second-guessing the surgeon and his work, and that was just not done. Also, if she had spoken up it could have endangered her future success in medical school.

The whole time Lee had put a brave face on the grim news. When I asked how she felt about her "50/50 chance," her reply shocked me. "That is all we can ever hope for in medicine. Only 50/50. We learn that in medical school." *Whaaat?* I thought, again stifling the anger and disappointment running through my mind.

As we drove home from the clinic, I watched Lee from my spot in the back seat. Once things got quiet, she began to cry. I could see her wiping the corners of her eyes with her headscarf. Although I had fought against my biases and assumptions all night, this time the mother in me was coming out and there was no stopping it.

"Forget being brave, Lee," I said. "Forget the 'suck it up and deal with it' cultural norm. For now, go ahead and cry. What you have been told is hugely disappointing."

I was shocked, outraged, and frustrated. A specialist in medicine had told a twenty-five-year old medical student who hadn't walked in almost five months that she would need to wait even longer, until "after the holidays." I was seething over the behavior of a seemingly uncaring human.

But I was even more angry and frustrated with God. He wasn't acting in accordance with my plan. Hadn't I laid my hands on Lee before we went into the clinic? Hadn't I prayed in the name of Jesus that she would walk out of that office feeling peaceful and with a plan that would have her walking again? Hadn't she agreed to pray with me, once again, knowing that I am a Christian who worships the Son of God?

Nothing that I had asked God to do had come about.

I thought, *C'mon God, work with me here. Did you see me trying to show Lee that you are a loving God who cares about what happens to us? And how you answer us when we call on your name, and how you are the Master Healer? Weren't you listening? How does it advance your cause when I pray like that and then she has a devastating experience like this? Why did you choose to be silent? What must Lee be thinking about you right now after the prayer I prayed and the experience she just had?*

Late that evening I went over the day's events with Curt. I vented my frustration, and once my soul was at rest again I remembered something. I immediately texted Lee and asked her to meet me the next day.

The next afternoon she sat across from me in a local café. I confessed my disappointment and frustration with God from the previous night. Then I told her a story that years ago had changed my perspective about prayer and God's timing. In 2000, my son, Jordan, was facing a second surgery to remove a rare and benign tumor from his cheek. (It had grown back quickly after having been removed the year before.) The doctor had said that the roots of Jordan's tumor were so small and so deep that he would not be able to remove it all; he would just try to get as much of it out as he could.

Jordan was only nine years old. I asked everyone I knew to pray for a miraculous healing. I even asked the Lord to use his healing power to shape my son's testimony at a very young age. Members of our extended family had experienced miraculous healings, and I wanted another one for my son. I wanted and expected the surgeon to walk out of the operating room following Jordan's surgery to announce: "Wow, I can't believe it. I actually got the entire tumor. I can't explain this."

After which I would say, "That's because Jesus healed him."

It was going to be a great story, but it didn't turn out according to my plan. Instead, the surgeon came out of the OR and said he was not able to get it all.

I was crushed. "Why God? Why didn't you give us the miracle we asked for? Why was my son having his second surgery and facing a lifelong battle with a rare tumor?"

That day in Chapel Hill, the surgeon, an expert in Jordan's particular kind of tumors, said, "The best-case scenario is that it will be three years before he needs another surgery. If he can go three years, I will be very happy."

I was telling this story to Lee in 2008 in a café in Southeast Asia. I looked her in the eyes and said, "That was eight years ago."

I explained that the tumor our son had is rare and very aggressive. It typically grows back over and over again because it has such deep roots. But for eight years the tumor in my son's cheek had not come back. It would have almost been forgotten were it not for a scraggly scar on the inside of my son's cheek that reminds him every day that God, not a doctor, healed him. And God most certainly did use this experience to craft Jordan's testimony, which he has given many times to many people.

God answered my prayer in a way that was so much more amazing and awesome than what I had originally asked for. His delayed answer caused me to first trust in His goodness, His power, and His perfect timing. But I had to wait many years to understand what really happened in the OR that day. Because God is not in the business of following our "to do" lists. He is far more interested in helping us learn how to trust Him.

I told Lee I knew that God really did hear my prayer for her the night before. All we needed to do was wait for His answer with the expectation that she would have a story of her own to tell one day. She nodded. In the midst of so much discouragement and frustration, I saw a glimpse of hope as her eyes filled with tears.

And still we waited. I prayed that God would heal her soul before He healed her knee. I wanted her to learn how to trust God, not to look at Him simply for what she could get out of Him. I wonder today how long it will take.

∞

It wasn't until a year after Lee's surgery that we learned that it had not been a specialist or even a board-certified doctor, but a medical student, who had performed the surgery on her knee. We also learned that the student doctor inserted the metal rod through a muscle in a way that caused permanent damage. Barring a miracle from God, Lee will never bend her knee again.

In her country, when things go wrong in the operating room a patient doesn't have any recourse. You can't question the doctor, and there is no legal avenue to pursue. What a Westerner would consider medical malpractice happens probably every day in this part of the world, and nothing can be done about it. When your chances are seen as only 50/50 anyway, an unfavorable outcome is simply accepted as God's will.

Unless God intervenes, the toes on the foot of Lee's injured leg will continue to curl. Occasionally she feels numbness and loses her balance and falls. The difficulties are intensified by the shame that her culture attributes to people with any kind of disability. Lee does not receive the respect she used to, and it's due entirely to the fact that she walks with a crutch and has a withered leg. This would be hard enough for a young woman architect to handle, but she is in medical school. In her province, you never see a doctor who has any type of physical disability.

Following the accident, she was told by her instructors in medical school that she could not continue in pediatrics until she was able to walk normally. She was given two choices for continuing her training, either train for the psychiatric hospital or the morgue. She chose the psychiatric hospital because, she told me, "at least I can talk to those patients."

This choice came with definite drawbacks. Culturally, a doctor assigned to the psychiatric hospital is considered at the bottom of the barrel. There isn't a great deal of psychiatric care available in her province, as the cultural approach to problems is to "think about something else." I knew to expect the worst when I visited her at that hospital, and I wasn't disappointed. Most of the patients were medicated and left alone, and there was just one doctor for the entire hospital.

Lee didn't work there very long before she became so discouraged she wanted to drop out of medical school. She had grown weary of comments from classmates that "the only reason you get good grades is because the teachers feel sorry for you." She also grew weary of the cultural belief that those who become disabled are being punished by Allah. It was strongly implied that she had done something horrible, and as a result somehow deserved to be disabled. The looks, the stares, the whispers just became too great a burden to bear.

In the midst of physical pain, heartbreak, and her interrupted career, I had many opportunities to speak truth into Lee's life. We had developed a wonderful older/younger sister connection, and she trusted me. She was fascinated at my own Father/child relationship with God, but didn't understand it. To her, God was someone whose favor you gain by doing good works and acts of "obligation." He certainly didn't feel like a personal, loving deity to her. But I saw that start to change.

"Why do you call God, 'Father'?" she asked. "Think about it," I said. "For one thing, He made me, right? He loves me, He comforts me, He knows what is best for me, He protects me, He teaches me, He disciplines me, He provides for me, He blesses me, and He forgives me when I tell Him I have done something wrong and I am sorry. Don't those all sound like things that a Father does for a child?"

She got it.

I shared with Lee how God uses all the experiences in our lives to mold us into the person He created us to be. I explained that God is an expert at taking tragedy and working it all out for good—that experiences such as hers are where He does His best work. He performs miracles, changes lives, and is expert at breathing life into dead situations. I told her that I believed that God was going to use this very painful time in her life to make her into an even better doctor than she could have been otherwise. She would know better than others how illness and broken bones can be life-changing experiences. I believed that through her accident and subsequent injury, God was calling her to Himself. And she understood that. She even agreed.

"Count it all joy my brothers when you meet trials of various kinds, for you know that the testing of your faith produces steadfastness. And let steadfastness have its full effect, that you may be perfect and complete, lacking in nothing." (James 1:2–4)

"Blessed is the man who remains steadfast under trial, for when he has stood the test, he will receive the crown of life which God has promised to those who love him." (James 1:12)

I wrote these verses from James out for Lee in English because she's a fluent speaker, and also wrote them in her native language. I wanted her to have these words from God in her heart language. I hoped that she would keep the verses and read them. My daughter, Molly, decorated the paper I wrote them out on so Lee would be more likely to use it as a bookmark or just hold on to it. I wasn't sure how she would receive it, because though she is a woman who wants to follow God, as I said, she is a Muslim. Although technically Muslims are permitted to read the Injil, or New Testament, I still was unsure how she would react because it was frowned upon in her culture. So I decided to let God's Word speak to her soul in a way that I couldn't. And as we should always expect, it did. Oh me of little faith!

When she read the verses she squealed and said, "I love it." Better yet, she kissed the paper and thanked me. She said that it gave her "much spirit." I was so moved by her reaction and that she revered God's Word so much that she actually kissed it. Had I ever seen one of my Christian friends do that?

God used these trials to open the door for me to talk to Lee about God's faithfulness. I told her the story of God's calling me and Curt and our children to work among Muslims following the tsunami. I mentioned that she and I would never have met if I had caved in to all the criticism I was hearing from friends and family back home. I told her how this applied to her life as well. Did she believe that God's calling on her life was to be a doctor, or was it just her parents' wishes? If it was from God, then she needed to stop paying attention to the lies that others were telling her and get back to school. When I said that, she cried. She needed someone to believe in her, just one person to encourage her and say, "You can do this!"

But I knew that my encouragement wasn't enough to get her back in school to stay. Sooner or later the pressure from the culture would get to her. She needed to find her calling and own it. She needed to lean on the one Person who would be able to give her the strength to continue on. She needed to own her relationship with God.

So I shared a verse: "For my grace is sufficient for you for my power is made perfect in weakness" (2 Corinthians 12:9). I wanted her to know this was an opportunity for her. "Let everyone watch and wonder where you get the joy and strength to continue in medical school when you have suffered a life-altering disability that your culture rejects. You have an opportunity to put your love for God and His power in and over your life on display! What a privilege to be chosen to show that to the world."

That was my pep talk and I meant every word of it. I also shared Jesus's parable about the house built on sand and the house built on the rock. "Everyone then who hears these words of mine and does them will be like a wise man who built his house on the rock. And the rain fell, and the floods came, and the winds blew and beat on that house, but it did not fall, because it had been founded on the rock. And everyone who hears these words of mine and does not do them will be like a foolish man who built his house on the sand. And the rain fell, and the floods came, and the winds blew and beat against that house, and it fell, and great was the fall of it" (Matthew 7:24–27).

If she tried to go back to school and endure the hardship in her own strength, she would not be able to stand up to the criticism she was sure to face. She needed to acknowledge that it was only because of the will of God and in the strength of God that she could continue. For the first time since her accident, I saw her face light up.

Lee's heart was changing and I could see that she was searching for the God who loved her and would stand by her. But even with determination and faith, her life would be a struggle. In public, people would ask what had happened to her—and their questions were not born out of compassion. It was easy to see the judgmental, condemning looks. I tried to amuse Lee by suggesting that each time it happens she make up an outrageous tale to help ease the stress.

We did laugh at times, but humor was not the answer to her pain. I told her about the story in John 9 where Jesus was asked if a man was born blind as a result of his own sin or that of his parents. Jesus cleared things up by saying "It was not that this man sinned, or his parents, but that the works of God might be displayed in him" (John 9:3).

Lee needed to believe God and the truth of that verse, rather than the lies of her culture. She chose to embrace the future instead of be condemned by her past—she returned to medical school, graduating in 2010. She can now say that Allah has taught her a lot through her accident and that it has made her a better doctor. She wasn't able to fulfill her parents' wish that she become a pediatrician, because of her disability. Instead she wants to start a volunteer program at the hospital, and she spends much of her free time doing something that other locals don't know how to do—comforting and encouraging patients. She learned that from the Body of Christ, when believers rallied around her at the time of her accident.

∞

During our three years together I shared the gospel and many Bible stories with Lee. She always asked good questions. (In her culture, people who ask questions about God and religion are considered "crazy.") We talked about how asking questions and being sure what you believe—and why you believe it—shows great spiritual strength and maturity. I could see that God was touching her life and breaking through the limitations imposed by her culture. I know that God can heal Lee's leg if He chooses to, but until then I am anxiously awaiting the day when her soul will be restored to Him. Whether she ever walks normally again, I will claim the promise of Romans 8:28 for her: "And we know that for those who love God all things work together for good, for those who are called according to his purpose."

Before I left Southeast Asia I challenged Lee again with the story of the blind man from John 9. Jesus made it clear that suffering does not result from our missteps, but is allowed by God so that we can glorify him. God reveals His strength in our weakness. But notice in

John 9:3 that Jesus used the word "might" rather than "would." "That the works of God might be displayed in him [the suffering person]." To me, that implies a choice on our part. Will we open our hearts so that God can move in our lives in the midst of suffering?

I don't know what He has planned for Lee. I only know that it wasn't an accident that she and I met. I know God is at work in Lee's heart…and that He isn't finished yet.

Chapter 19

MUCH MORE THAN MY HELPER

When God Doesn't Show Up Like You Expected

Without a doubt, my closest friend in Southeast Asia was my house helper, Natalie. While it may sound luxurious to have had a house helper, it is expected that Western families will have household help. In fact, for our family to *not* have a helper would have reflected poorly on us. We would have been seen as a family who chose not to provide a local with a well-paying job.

And beyond the dictates of local custom, for us it was a basic necessity because daily living in that part of the world is so much harder. Our home, like most, was not equipped with a dishwasher, clothes dryer, vacuum, central air conditioning, or other conveniences that Westerners rely on every day. We could only afford to air condition our bedrooms, so we had to keep the windows open throughout the house, which meant every inch of the interior was constantly coated with dirt. Every day we had to sweep and mop the entire house.

Natalie helped keep us ahead of the dirt, the chores, and the fatigue of enduring constant heat and oppressive humidity. Her services were inexpensive by Western standards, and by hiring her we were providing her family with their only means of steady income. For the equivalent of $100 U.S. a month, I had someone who would clean my house, cook traditional meals from scratch, and iron clothes from eight to one, Monday through Friday. I'm not going to lie, it was wonderful.

I decided from the beginning, though, that I wanted our helper to be more than just hired help. I wanted to know this woman. I wanted to be her friend.

Natalie provided motivation to learn the language quickly because I didn't want to just smile and say "Thank you" and nothing more to her. Although she was not my formal language tutor, she became my greatest teacher because she was in our home every day. She saw us at our best and our worst. I laughingly wondered if she was becoming a little too familiar with us when she would come in first thing and see me sitting at the table in my pajamas, with bed head, and remark with the painful honesty so common in her culture: "Ohh, you're not beautiful yet."

God was so faithful to me in this relationship, because, to be honest, when I first met Natalie I didn't really like her. A teammate had introduced us, knowing that Natalie needed a job. She was standoffish at first, unlike most of the locals we had met. And our being friendly didn't work to break the ice with Natalie. Still, we needed a helper so we hired her and later we laughed about my initial instincts and first impressions being so wrong.

It wasn't until later that I found out why she was so guarded, and even a little afraid, at our first meeting. She had previously worked for a different American family that had not treated her well. She didn't know if we might treat her poorly, and she later told me she wasn't even sure she wanted the job.

On her first day, before I had even a working knowledge of her language, all I could do was smile and say "good morning" and "thank you." I wanted to interact more with her so I asked my language tutor to help me learn how to say something different to Natalie every day. For starters, I asked my tutor how to say "Do your kids like school?" In the morning when Natalie would come in, I'd try out my latest memorized attempt at conversation. I must have pulled it off because she would launch into a conversation, most of which I couldn't understand. But after weeks of listening, I started to understand bits and pieces of what she was telling me. I kept learning and practicing, and after a few months we were having conversations that actually went back and forth.

I'll never forget one of my first opportunities to share Truth with her that first spring. Although we were living under Shari'a law, the country officially recognized five religions. All citizens were required to claim one of the five and have that listed on their national identification card, which they were required to carry everywhere they went. Although the people group in our province were Muslim, elsewhere in the country citizens were identified as either a Muslim, Catholic, Protestant, Buddhist, or Hindu.

Oddly, in our strict Muslim province, Easter, Christmas, and Ascension Day were recognized as holidays on the calendar. Natalie was surprised on Good Friday when I told her that preparing lunch that day was not necessary because we were fasting. That launched into a discussion of why we were doing that as I explained the meaning of Good Friday and Easter. It was in that conversation that I experienced firsthand the truth of Romans 10:14,

How then can they call on the one they have not believed in? And how can they believe in the one of whom they have not heard?

And how can they hear without someone preaching to them?

How can they preach unless they are sent?

She had heard about Good Friday, perhaps from seeing it on a calendar. She did not seem surprised when I told her that was the day Jesus had been crucified. Had she heard that before, or were my new language skills not as sharp as I thought? Perhaps it was the assumption that of course Prophet Jesus was dead, because the prophet that she followed was. But no one had ever told her the rest of the story. When I told her about what happened three days later, she gasped. "Oh yeah? He became alive again?"

She had never heard! And so on Good Friday, Natalie heard the gospel for the first time.

She was thirty-four when we met. At fifteen she had been forced by her mother into an unwanted marriage. Although she was in middle school and was a good student when she got married, she had to drop out at sixteen when she became pregnant. Now eighteen years later, she had a son a year younger than mine, a daughter a year older than mine, and she had lost a three-year old son to a cancerous tumor. Sadly this was not the first great loss in her life.

When she was just three years old, she lost her only sibling, an older sister. The nature of her family relationships were such that when I asked what her deceased sister's name was, she didn't know. After all these years, she no longer remembered. Two years after she lost her only sibling, her father died when Natalie was just five. So in a culture that places a high value on having a big family, it had been just Natalie and her mother until she was married off at fifteen. Now that she was an adult, married with two living children, she desperately wanted another child.

After months of trying, hoping, and waiting, in July 2007 Natalie got pregnant. By this time, our relationship had progressed to a real friendship. Most days we would spend a great deal of time talking while she worked, and into the late afternoon after her duties were completed. We had grown close, so I was the first person she told about her pregnancy. However my joy turned to horror as I watched her fast during the month of Ramadan, which fell during her first trimester. Though she continued to work, she wouldn't eat or drink anything, not even water, from sunup to sundown. I tried to explain how dangerous that was for the baby, but she assured me that she was strong enough and had done it before.

In Islam, pregnant women are excused from fasting during Ramadan, but they are expected to make it up at another time. And frankly, it's a lot harder to fast for a month when you're the only one doing it. I told Natalie that if she wouldn't even drink water, then she was not allowed to sweep and mop my house until the fasting month was over. I told her that I would do it. She thought that was silly, but I couldn't stand by and watch her do hard, sweaty work that was dangerous for her baby.

As the months passed, Natalie never talked about her pregnancy. What pregnant woman doesn't love to talk with a close friend about that? And though I had never seen her pregnant before, I didn't think she looked like someone who was expecting, let alone her fourth child. She wasn't very big to start with, and when I would ask her to stand sideways and pull her dress tight so I could admire her growing belly (a request she found very strange but she obliged me anyway), something didn't look right. When I would force conversation about it, she confessed her fears of the baby not surviving. I knew she was afraid to lose another child.

Natalie believed in God's sovereignty in all things. In Islam, ev-

erything that happens is seen as God's will. To calm her fears about
losing her baby, I encouraged her to trust God with this pregnancy in
a way she never had before. When I took her for an ultrasound at six
months, the image was so blurry I couldn't make out much more than
the baby's torso. I certainly didn't see ten fingers and toes or a head.
The midwife said everything was normal, but I had doubts.

I felt that I was the only one who was questioning how things were
done. Once again I had to lay down my own culture, trust that the
midwife knew what she was seeing, and hope that everything was fine.
Besides, I told myself, *the image was of such poor quality because the ultrasound machine was probably very outdated.*

Unlike women in the West who usually have their husbands beside them when they give birth, in this culture women typically are
attended by their older sister. Since Natalie didn't have one, she invited
me to be her older sister. I was so honored and very excited about being
beside her on one of the most important days of her life. She stopped
working at our house in late February to remain at home in anticipa-
tion of the birth in early April. However, on the morning of March 17,
about two weeks before her due date, I got a text message that stopped
me in my tracks.

It was from Natalie's sister-in-law. "Did you know that Natalie's
baby is dead?" read the message.

I hadn't heard that Natalie had gone into labor or that the baby
had been born. After all, we had planned for me to be with her. How
could I be hearing about a death?

I threw my clothes on and Curt drove me to Natalie's house.
There was a lot of activity around their traditional house in a rural village. Natalie hadn't returned home from the midwife's, where she had
given birth, but the baby's body had already been brought to the house.
Older women from the village were squatting beside a fire over which

they were boiling water. Neighbors were standing around, and yet I don't remember hearing any conversation. It was crowded but silent. Everyone had serious, dazed looks on their faces. Though some came to greet me, no one said anything. We did the traditional greeting of touching hands and women touching cheeks on either side, but in silence.

I spotted Natalie's thirteen-year old daughter standing alone. She was normally a little shy, and I could tell she was conflicted about seeing me. She had such a pained expression that her face looked pale and drawn. Our eyes met and she disappeared in to the house, reappearing a few minutes later with her father. Natalie's husband greeted me and I could tell he was in busy mode, attempting to cover his grief with activity. And yet the pain in his eyes was palpable. What I didn't know at the time was that he and other men had been digging a grave behind the house.

He told me that Natalie was still at the midwife's, but did I want to see the baby's body? I politely declined, telling him I wanted to get to Natalie as soon as possible. He directed their teenage son to hop on his motorbike and lead the way through the densely wooded village to the midwife's house.

Curt and I, along with one of Natalie's relatives who had jumped in our car, followed Natalie's son to the midwife's house. Still in shock myself, I was silently praying and trying to prepare myself for what I might find there. We rode past cows, sheep, goats, leafy banana trees, and people going about their usual daily routine on a Monday morning. Then we pulled up to a simple, older house. I tried to prepare for the worst.

Chapter 20

CHALLENGING A CULTURAL BLIND SPOT

When God Was Silent I Decided to Speak Up

I opened the door to the midwife's house, momentarily closing my eyes against the dirty walls. I swallowed hard as I took in the overall rundown look that was just as disturbing on the inside as it was on the outside. But everything else fell out of focus as Natalie held out her arms to me, an unusual thing to do in her culture.

I had never seen true anguish on someone's face until then. She was so grief-stricken she looked like a different person. We said nothing at first, just embraced and cried. As I held her, my body was shaking with shock and grief. I wanted to be strong for Natalie, but in that moment I couldn't. She kept saying the words "only for a moment" over and over in her native tongue. That's all she'd had with her baby, the child she had wanted for so long.

Natalie's relative, who was present in the room, simply said to me, "I'm going to go home now." There was no compassion or tenderness in the woman's eyes. Instead I think she was relieved that someone else had come so she could leave.

Natalie had planned to have another ultrasound that day, but she hadn't slept well and back labor began that morning. Her contractions weren't very regular so she wasn't expecting to deliver the baby. But fifteen minutes after she arrived at the midwife's home the baby was on his way. There had been no time to call me.

Her baby didn't cry when he was born; he made only a very faint sound. The midwife said he was weak. She cleaned him up and allowed Natalie to hold him just for a minute. It was the only minute she would have with him. When the baby failed to respond in a typical, healthy way, it was decided that Natalie's husband and the midwife would take the baby to a nearby hospital. By the time they arrived there the baby was dead. As quickly as he came he was gone.

A relative was called to bring Natalie's husband and baby back to the house, where the body was prepared for burial in accordance with Muslim tradition. Natalie, still alone at the midwife's home and unaware of what was happening, never saw or held her newborn son again.

As the morning went by, I took in the thin rubber mattress on the bed, covered only with a traditional sarong that Natalie had brought from home. I noted the unlit room that had no sink, no soap, and certainly no hand sanitizer. Then there was the bowl of dirty, bloody water on the floor beneath the bed. I wondered why Natalie had to lose her son, and in such primitive and unsanitary surroundings.

I felt ashamed that just because I was born in the West, I was given seemingly preferential treatment in life. That felt very, very unfair.

As Curt and I tried to comfort Natalie, the midwife would occasionally enter the room and ask Natalie if she was in pain. As she attended to her physical needs, I noticed the midwife's attention was directed out the window. As she pressed on Natalie's abdomen there was no compassion; she was just going through the motions. You would never have known she was attending to a patient who was grieving after having lost her baby. At one point the midwife almost knocked over one of the bowls of bloody water on the floor, but she showed no alarm. Instead she finished with Natalie, put another bowl of bloody water on the floor, and walked out.

I stood there wondering where all the blood was coming from. From Natalie? From a previous patient? How long had they been sitting there?

I had lived in country long enough to no longer be shocked by the comparatively poor sanitation in settings where a person was seeking medical care. But still I found it hard to accept. Knowing what my Natalie had been through that morning, I felt a persistent lump in my throat.

I sat by her side, holding her hand, talking and crying with her, listening to her, rubbing a wet towel on her face and neck, giving her sips of water, doing anything I could to comfort my dear, heartbroken friend.

Most of the time it was just the two of us in the room. We managed to have some meaningful conversations in the midst of tremendous shock and grief. Natalie said, "Everything is in God's hands. We don't know how long any of us has here. We don't know how long we will have with any of our children. And this one God meant for me to have only for a moment."

As I held her hand and listened, the *whys* and the *what ifs* kicked in. Would her baby have lived had Natalie been cared for in a First World hospital? Why is it that death is so easily accepted here? What really happened earlier that morning? Why does no one here look squarely at the situation and seek an honest answer when something like this happens?

As the morning wore on, neighbors and relatives came in and out of Natalie's room. It was always the same conversation. They would ask, "What happened?" and then listen as she relayed her story.

The visitors and their indifferent manner showed a lack of real concern. "Are you feeling sick? Are you in pain?" They spoke bluntly, and I never saw anyone embrace Natalie or pray for her. I stayed next to her, holding her hand, wishing I could bring her baby back. I had spent months encouraging Natalie to trust God with her fears. She had wanted this child so badly and had worried that it would not survive, while I encouraged her to trust and believe. Now the baby was dead and her arms were empty.

Inside I was wrestling with God. I had pictured the joy we would all share as Natalie gave birth to her fourth child. I imagined her holding the baby as we ooohed and aaaahed over him. I imagined long, deep conversations about the blessings of turning your fears over to the Lord and allowing him to carry your burdens. But instead, I had walked into a nightmare at the midwife's home. Natalie was distraught, her heart and hopes crushed, and I was the only person trying to support and comfort her. I knew God had a purpose in this, but I definitely wasn't seeing it...yet.

Later in the morning Natalie's husband arrived with food. He lovingly served her and seemed genuinely concerned about her condition. But as she ate, I saw him too look out the window. His eyes were so sad; he looked absolutely lost. Was he wondering how life could seem so normal outside when in that room, his world had come crashing down? It wasn't long before he announced that he needed to return to their house "to prepare for the guests." He asked Curt and me to bring Natalie home when she was ready. Another woman was in the next room, laboring with her first child. I hoped Natalie would be ready to go home before the woman next door gave birth. I didn't want her to hear the sound of a baby's loud, healthy cry.

Around 3 p.m., the midwife released Natalie. She was unsteady on her feet, more a result of her grief than physical pain. She and I sat in the back seat of the car, and I held her hand and choked back tears. Few words were spoken. She was in a daze. We arrived at her home, where Curt took hold of one of Natalie's arms and I grabbed the other. We slowly ascended the steep, cement stairs that led to her front door, only to be stared at by all the neighbors who had gathered at her home.

But no one came to our assistance. Neighbors and family members that weren't staring and whispering simply carried on conversations as Curt and I helped her into her bedroom.

I wasn't prepared for what I saw inside the house that day. Just as the locals would do on high holy days in Islam, all the furniture had been moved out of the living room, rugs were laid down on the floors, and jars of traditional snacks were lined up. It was exactly how you would find a home set up to welcome guests on the holiday after the fasting month.

The room was full of people dressed in their best clothes. It felt like a holiday, and that made me angry. I wanted to take Natalie to my house, put her in my more comfortable bed, turn on the AC, hold her hand, and let her sleep, or talk, whatever she needed. Instead, there she was, still in shock, still feeling contractions, with ten people conversing loudly in her front room while eating snacks and drinking traditional syrupy drinks. They acted as if it were a holiday.

We brought Natalie into her bedroom and laid her down on a lumpy mattress in her sweltering bedroom. There wasn't even a fan we could turn on. I sat by her side and held her hand, stroking her hair, while a parade of guests came in and out of her room. They were asking the same questions we had heard at the midwife's: "What happened? Do you feel sick?"

An hour later, Natalie's mother finally entered the room. It was the first time she was seeing her daughter after the traumatic events earlier that morning. She walked in, looked at her grieving daughter, and asked, "Are you in pain?"

Then she left the room to attend to the guests. No words of comfort, no touch, no embrace. I couldn't believe the complete absence of love. Was I imposing my own culture on to the situation, and assuming mine was "better"?

∞

I sat beside Natalie on the bed, holding her hand as a parade of people came through the house. Some would come into the room, and some would stay in the front room and eat the snacks. Most asked about what had happened, but as they listened to the details, their faces were expressionless. Once they got the information they were seeking, they would change the subject to talk about the rice fields or a brother who had had surgery or a sister's husband who had taken a second wife.

As many left, they slipped envelopes of money into Natalie's hand. Throughout the day and into the night, I never heard any prayers said for her, never saw an embrace. I saw nothing that communicated love or concern as I understand it.

At one point, Natalie's mother returned with an aunt to take Natalie to another room for a bath. I excused myself and set out to find Natalie's teenage daughter, who was a year older than Molly. I hadn't seen her since that glimpse I'd had when I arrived at the home that morning. I knew that her daughter, Fiona, had not seen her mother that day, even though we had been back at Natalie's home for a few hours. I couldn't help but think about my own daughter and how she wouldn't have left my side if I had been the one to lose a baby.

I found Fiona huddled in the kitchen. I reached out to hug her.

The normally shy girl returned my hug and started bawling in my arms. We didn't talk. I just held her. She was trying so hard to put on a brave face. And yet there was no denying that she was just a broken-hearted teenager trying to deal with a profound loss. After we embraced, she turned to go outside without saying a word. She disappeared out the door alone, still crying.

A neighbor asked if I wanted some food. I declined, explaining that I needed to get back to Natalie.

"Why not eat something?" the woman asked. "Natalie is fine!"

I wanted to be respectful of this neighbor, who was a relative of Natalie's. So I said in as polite but firm a way as possible, "I disagree with you. Her baby died this morning. That is a huge loss for her. I do not agree that she is 'fine'." The woman gave me a puzzled look, understanding the words but not understanding the meaning behind them.

I stayed by Natalie's side until the sunset Muslim prayer time, when I asked if I could pray for her before I left. Although Natalie is a Muslim and I am a Christian, she loved it when I would pray for her. It was something we often did together. Even though Muslims pray with their eyes open and palms held up and out, when I would pray for her she would close her eyes and bow her head like me. I would say "amen" when I was finished, and she would as well, and then wipe her face with her hands, as Muslims typically do, signifying a desire to receive God's blessing.

As I prepared to go home, I promised her I would walk this road beside her, that she was not alone, and that when she was with me she didn't have to be brave. I told her that God wasn't mad when she was sad, that He wanted her to give her sadness to Him so that He could show her how much He loves her. And that He would comfort her in a way that no one else could. We hugged and I told her I loved her.

When I got home, I just cried. Why did this have to happen?

After the loss of Natalie's third child two years before, I knew they had really wanted this baby. Because she was so afraid of losing the baby, for six months she had told only two people that she was pregnant—her husband and me. She had already suffered so much loss. Why did her baby have to die?

Chapter 21

RELYING ON GOD WHEN
NOTHING MAKES SENSE

God Shows, Again, That During the Hardest Times, He Can Work Miracles

The hardest day of the three years I lived in Southeast Asia was the day Natalie's baby died. It hurt me to see someone I love be so dismissed in the midst of her pain. How could her culture be so void of compassion? It wasn't until later that I realized maybe God was opening a door for me.

I also realized, later, that Satan was using my anger and disillusionment to feed my cynicism about the people and their ways. Satan told me things like "Doesn't this culture drive you crazy? Look at them! Where is the love?! How can you love these people who are sooo cold?"

I went back to Natalie's home first thing the following morning. She was standing outside in the doorway at the top of the cement stairs. I commented on how much stronger she seemed, and I meant physically stronger. She said, "Oh yes, I am not thinking about it anymore." I could see that her culture had gotten hold of her heart in the short time we had been apart.

I tried to explain that thinking about her traumatic loss was normal. If she tried to pretend it hadn't happened or that it didn't matter, her heart would be sick. I told her that women she had met, and some that she had never met, were praying for her back in the States. I told her that one of my friends back home had her small group from church praying for her all day.

She smiled and said, "Oh thank you." But still there was a strange distance between us. She wasn't the raw, transparent Natalie that she had been the day before. She was being as cold and aloof as the guests who had invaded her house.

It was as if Natalie was numb. All that day, just like the previous one, guests arrived, eating snacks and chit-chatting, while she lay on the bed and smiled and made small talk.

I knew that deep down she was deeply grieved. But I could see that to survive in her culture, she had to shut down. There was tremendous pressure to just forget about it. I'm so thankful that God loves us and knows us so intimately and that He gave us feelings and is glorified when we give our heartbreak to Him and allow Him to heal us.

I wanted Natalie to experience God's healing. I wanted her to be able to say: "I am healed because God comforted me in such a personal and intimate way that no one else could. Because He is a faithful God, He has used my pain to teach me something that made me love Him, trust Him, believe Him, and know Him more through this experience that I never could have learned otherwise."

Even though I was frustrated that her religion offered her no hope, I knew God was working through her painful situation. I knew that many times people meet Christ when they come to the end of themselves. And I knew that God could use her stories of incredible loss to craft an amazing testimony about who He is and how He changes lives. God promises us: "I will turn their mourning into gladness; I will give them comfort and joy instead of sorrow" (Jeremiah 31:13).

The following day, Wednesday, I found Natalie lying in bed with her husband beside her. She was weeping. Her breast milk had come in and she was engorged and suffering terrible pain. Her husband was concerned. I asked Natalie's daughter for some hot water and towels. I spent that day putting warm compresses on Natalie, desperately trying to make her more comfortable. As I dipped the towels in the scalding water, over and over, frequently changing out the ones that had grown cold, we talked. And she really shared her heart. Natalie was back.

We discussed the need for Natalie and her husband to talk together about their loss, to cry together, and not let their relationship become distant. She said that her husband had regrets. He wished they had chosen to have the baby at a hospital instead of the midwife's so they would have been closer to the next level of medical care. She said she had chosen that particular midwife because she was "good, but also the least expensive."

My heart sank. I told her I was sure they had done all they could to save their son. We talked about the fragility of life, about how we can't understand the ways of God, but we can always trust that He is good, even in the midst of situations that don't make sense to us. God is God and we are not. As I changed the towels and the day went on, she started to feel better.

I prayed over her. "Thank you, Lord, for giving me this chance to serve Natalie, to truly wash her feet. Show me how to really love and serve her, to show her gospel love like she has never seen."

Once again, people came in and out of the house. Once again, they showed no compassion. That is, until something amazing happened.

∞

I went home in the late afternoon, to return later that evening with a special guest to surprise Natalie. It was my friend Lee, who had been seriously injured the year before in a motorbike accident. Lee was one of my language teachers, and she and Natalie became friends back when Lee was frequently in my home.

When Lee heard about Natalie's loss, she said, "I need to visit her, to talk to her."

Lee went straight to Natalie's bedroom, sat on the bed, and held Natalie's hand. Moments later a new set of guests arrived. A large group of women came into the room, gave Natalie a quick traditional greeting, then went into the front room for snacks. Lee and I were asked to join them, which we needed to do in order to be polite. Unlike previous days, this time Natalie encouraged both of us to sit with her guests. As I looked into Natalie's room through an open door, I was pained to see her lying there alone. Lee seized the opportunity to leave the guests and returned to Natalie's side.

She rubbed Natalie's legs and they talked and talked. Lee had just learned that she would never again bend her knee. She would walk with a crutch for the rest of her life, barring a miracle. Her disability had destroyed her plan to become the pediatrician she and her parents had hoped she would be. I could see what a great bedside manner this future doctor had. To witness these two precious women, who have endured great suffering, holding hands, loving each other like sisters, drawing comfort and strength from each other was amazing.

By now hundreds of guests had come through the house, but Lee was the first person I had seen touch Natalie and show love and compassion. As we left, Natalie got up and looked like herself again. The tired expression was gone, and the warm face that I love was there. In the car on the way home I thanked Lee for being so loving with Natalie. And then she said, "All of you showed me how to do that. You helped me so much when I had my accident. So I wanted to do for her what you all did for me."

There were more miracles to come. Loving Natalie through the painful loss of her baby led to big changes. In the days following her baby's death, she told me, "I have wanted a sister for so long. I have prayed for God to give me one. You are the sister that I prayed for."

I was speechless. Even more amazing, she told me, "The people in my village are very suspicious of white Westerners. But they see you, the way you dress, how polite you are, and how you took care of me. Now they see you are a good person. Now they trust you."

I had done nothing extraordinary. I was just doing what came naturally as a follower of Jesus. That's when I realized how absolutely powerful a transformed life communicates Christ in a place that has never had a gospel witness.

Natalie and I had many great conversations in those grief-filled days. We talked about how God is always good, in every situation and in every heartache. We said how much we wish her baby had lived, but that though we could not understand God's plan, we knew that someday we would see His hand in it somehow. Every life has a purpose, even one that was only lived for a few minutes. We agreed that we can't always understand God's ways because we are only human, we aren't God. We knew that God was also intentional in bringing the two of us together.

Natalie had wanted a sister, so God had put me there to be with her in her time of greatest need and deepest grief. What an honor.

Chapter 22

A Second Chance for Glen

God Keeps Sending the Right People into Your Life

In addition to Natalie and Lee, other locals were in our home every day, especially in the first six months. Our language tutors were native to the area, yet were fluent English speakers. When we first met one of them, a man named Glen, we would not have predicted that he would become one of our closest friends.

At twenty-three, Glen was pursuing a bachelor's degree at the local university. Though he was studying chemical engineering, once I got to know him he confessed that he would prefer to be an artist. But most college students there take an exam to get into college, and the school assigns their course of study. Or, like Lee, their parents decide their major.

When we first met Glen, he was very, very guarded. I tried to break the ice by asking if he would share his tsunami story with us, because I knew every local had a story to tell.

He opened up enough to describe a horrendous ordeal. "The

night before the tsunami, several friends and I spent the night at our friend's house at the beach. In the morning, we woke up to do our sunrise prayers. As we were doing our *wudu* (the ritual washing that Muslims perform before saying their prayers), I noticed that my friend's face looked like it was shining. I didn't know why, I just remember thinking that.

"After our prayers, we all went back to sleep. We woke up again during the earthquake. Everything was falling off the walls. It was the biggest earthquake any of us had ever been in. When it stopped, we all decided that we would go home and check on our families. I left on my motorcycle and I never saw my friend again, because his entire village was lost in the tsunami. Now I know why his face was shining that morning. He was getting ready to meet Allah."

Wow. I asked Glen how he felt about coming so close to dying. If he, like his friend, had stayed at the beach we wouldn't be having that conversation. He paused and said, "I feel lucky."

"Why do you feel lucky?" I asked.

"Because I have another chance. I have another chance to make things right with Allah," he said.

"Yes Glen, you do," I said.

But it might not be in the way that you think, I thought. For six months we spent five days a week, 9 o'clock to noon, with Glen. Over time he began to share more about his life. He considered us to be something like his second parents, and he enjoyed just hanging out as friends too. He taught us more about local culture than anyone. He was always so patient with our questions, and we had developed a lot of trust that enabled him to be transparent with us.

Eventually we realized that we knew more about his daily life than his family did. We had learned that although the Muslims we knew had very good community, something was missing. They did everything together and had a strong sense of looking out for one another. When someone got married, the entire village helped with preparations and joined in the festivities. Can you imagine your entire American subdivision working together to prepare food and coordinate all aspects of one resident's wedding? Of course not. We are far too individualistic for that to happen. However, as tight as their communities were in this province, the interpersonal relationships tended to be rather shallow. There was a clear quid pro quo approach to relationship.

Glen had never before had someone ask him on a regular basis, "How was your day?" or "How did your test go?" I could tell that he enjoyed the connection he had with our family. It wasn't long before he started texting us and answering questions before we had a chance to ask.

"Hey, I passed my test!" or "I have an interview today at 9:00. Please pray for me."

From the start, we established ourselves as people who pray and who talk about God. We wanted the local people to see us as we really are. Although many Muslims falsely believe that Christians worship three Gods, because of their misunderstanding of the triune nature of God, we found that in the context of friendship our Muslim friends never turned down our offer to pray for them. And, as was the case with Glen and others, it wasn't long before they began requesting prayer.

∞

One morning Glen showed up for our language lesson, but he was uncharacteristically early. (What can you expect from a culture that has an oft-used phrase that translates to "rubber time?") We never expected a session of language study with Glen to start on time.

So it was a shock when, one morning about 8:30, Curt heard the familiar sound of a motorbike outside our front gate. The kids and I were still getting ready in our rooms, savoring the last few moments before heading out into the sweltering heat that was the rest of our house.

Curt, meanwhile, was sitting in the front room reading The Return of the Prodigal Son, by Henri Nouwen. Glen came in and he and Curt began to catch up. Alone, just one-on-one, Glen seemed relaxed and in a curious mood. Within minutes, he looked down at the Henri Nouwen book. "What are you reading, Mr. Curt?"

Over the next thirty minutes, Curt and Glen talked through Luke 15:11-32, the parable of the prodigal son. First, Glen studied the Rembrandt painting on the front of the book while Curt recounted the story of the young man who had squandered his inheritance and finally returned home to his forgiving father.

In a culture that is so intent on masking anything that might bring shame or embarrassment, Glen was intrigued by the depiction of the loving father laying hands on his disgraced son. An artist at heart himself, Glen remained silent as he stared at the painting.

Curt got up and pulled two Bibles from our bookshelf, one in English and the other in the local language. Unsure that Glen would be willing to even touch it because he was a very conservative Muslim, Curt extended the Bible that was translated into Glen's language.

"Rather than my telling you the story, let me show you how Isa (the Arabic name for Jesus) told the story."

Glen took the Bible and, together, he and Curt read the incredible story of sin, repentance, forgiveness, and grace. After reading the story, they talked about its meaning—how we often behave like the elder son, self-righteous and selfish. How the younger son thought little about the shame he had brought on his father until he realized he had nowhere else to go. And how the prodigal son did nothing to deserve the grace and mercy he received from his father.

As he told the story, Curt explained who Christ is, why He came, and what it all means. For the first time, Glen heard the gospel, and all because he showed up thirty minutes early for language class.

It was the first of many times that Glen heard the Truth.

∞

One evening several weeks later, we wanted to present Glen with a UNC basketball T-shirt. Although basketball isn't as popular there as it is in the States, Glen played on a local team which, eventually, he invited Curt and Jordan to join. He had become a Tarheels fan after we invited him to watch a Duke-Carolina game on satellite TV. We'd been trying to give the T-shirt to him as a surprise, but hadn't seen him in a few days.

Curt received a text: "Hey, what are you guys doing? Can I come to your house?"

It was a Sunday night. Glen's village was a thirty-minute ride away and we didn't usually get together on Sunday nights, especially since we would see him the following morning for language study. We wondered if he knew about the T-shirt. When he arrived, he asked to speak to Curt alone. There was an urgency in his voice.

I wondered: "Maybe he has some serious spiritual questions to ask, especially after the prodigal son conversation!"

But that wasn't it. One of the inevitable moments that Westerners experience when working cross-culturally, and one of the most difficult to discern, is when we are asked for money. That night Glen asked Curt if he could borrow the equivalent of $500 US. He said he had an investment opportunity that he wanted to take advantage of. "I will be able to pay you back half of it in a week, and the rest of it within three months. But I need the money right away."

Curt was suspicious, of course. Pyramid schemes are common in

the Third World, where people are susceptible to get-rich-quick opportunities. This scam involved selling a product called Bio Disc,
which claimed to do everything from cure cancer to make water taste
better. (The latter was not a bad pitch in a land where the only clean
water is bottled!).

We knew this discussion could make or break our relationship
with Glen, and Curt knew what to do. He asked, "Glen, have you
talked to your parents about this?"

"No," he replied.

"OK. I always feel uneasy about doing something that you don't t
feel comfortable discussing with your parents. Before I make a decision, I want to do some research on this company, this product, and
this investment opportunity. If I find out it's legitimate, then I'll pray
about whether God wants me to be the one to loan you the money.

"But a bad investment or a crooked company is a dangerous thing
for you to get involved in. I don't want to see you get hurt, and I don't
want to see any relationships you have be damaged by your involving
others in a potentially bad investment. Give me twenty-four hours and
I will get back to you."

Glen agreed and thanked Curt. The next day they talked again,
and Curt showed Glen what he had found on the Internet. Bio Disc
was a scam. Glen was a little disappointed, but he looked Curt in the
eye and said, "Thank you. I can see that you really care about me."

What Satan meant for evil and confusion, God used for good. In
a situation where we could have lost a great friend and our best language tutor, and where we were making inroads to share the gospel,
our bond with Glen was made stronger. He could see that we did not
act out of duplicity or with false motives, but only out of concern for
him. In a culture rife with corruption, that was highly unusual and
incredibly powerful.

Throughout our remaining time in Southeast Asia, we spent many hours with Glen. He became part of our family, celebrating the kids' birthdays with us, going snorkeling with us, and learning to love pancakes. The power of the witness of a strong Christian family is just incredible to someone who has never before experienced the love of authentic Christian community. Though we had read book after book about sharing the gospel with Muslims, the four of us spending time and sharing life with Glen was the best witnessing tool we had.

Bishop Stephen Neill, an Anglican missionary, bishop, and scholar from Scotland once said,

> Within the fellowship of those who are bound together by personal loyalty to Jesus Christ, the relationship of love reaches an intimacy and intensity unknown elsewhere. Friendship between the friends of Jesus of Nazareth is unlike any other friendship. This ought to be normal experience within the Christian community…where it is experienced, especially across the barriers of race, nationality and language, it is one of the most convincing evidences of the continuing evidences of the continuing activity of Jesus among men."[2]

When it came time for us to leave our home in Southeast Asia, parting with Glen was one of the hardest friendships for us to leave. He is by nature a shy person and not confident expressing his emotions. Yet on our last night he sent a heartfelt text. We were at the airport awaiting our flight, furiously texting final goodbye messages to our friends. Glen's text appeared: "Meeting your family was the best

---

2. Bishop Stephen Neill, *Christian Faith Today* (New Orleans, La.: Pelican, 1955), 174.

experience of my life. When I have a family, I want it to be just like yours.'

God is always intentional with the people He brings into our lives. None of our relationships are coincidental; He has purpose in all of them. The question is "what are we doing with these relationships?" Are we telling the people we meet and get to know about Jesus? Are we afraid that the "news that changes everything" may offend them? Why do we say "God sees everything, He is in control of all things" and then act as if He isn't involved in who He brings into our lives?

Our relationship with Glen, and the way we saw God transform his heart in a relatively short time, taught us that God has intention and purpose in every relationship. And that changed everything.

Chapter 23

THE POWER OF A CHRISTIAN'S PRESENCE

Your Life Can Be a Convincing Witness of God's Transforming Work

I was made to live in a culture that values the connections within a community. Nothing communicates "I love you" to me like someone spending time with me. And in 2006, God sent me to live in a culture where the universal love language is quality time.

While community was everything in Southeast Asia, relationships tended to be shallow. So the power of an incarnational witness was a remarkable thing to see. One morning I spent time with Natalie learning how to cook some of my favorite local dishes. Her mother was going on the pilgrimage to Mecca that year, something everyone in this strict Muslim province wanted to do once in their life. Before her journey to Saudi Arabia, a feast would be prepared. Natalie invited me to join in on the cooking that would be done by all the women in the village.

When I told her I was honored to be invited, Natalie said, "Everyone wants you to come. They said you are very different."

"Why do they say that?"

"When my baby died, you wanted to get to me right away. You said that was the most important thing, and they said how out of the ordinary that was. They saw you give me so much attention. You come to our weddings and homes and you eat our food and drink our drinks. They see the way you dress, that you wear a head scarf. You're not like the other foreigners. They like that you are so polite."

Although I had learned a lot about the importance of being "like them" as much as possible to bridge cultural boundaries, I guess this was the first time I realized how much it had made an impression on those around me. Suddenly, all of the times I was hot and miserable wearing my head scarf were totally worth it.

Most of the time when I was out in public, I was aware of being "on display." I could feel strangers' eyes on everything I did, what I said, how I sat, how I prayed, how I ate, what I ate, how I dressed. But because I was on display, I was putting the gospel on display as well, for the very first time in the lives of most of the people in our city. Sometimes we think we have to have all the right words and all the verses memorized so we can share the gospel. And we assume we have to wait for God to open a door for us to share about Him. Sure we need to always be prepared to give the reason for the hope that we have, but living an incarnational life is a powerful witness too.

An incarnational life displays gospel transformation to the world because the Bible says that when we know Christ, we become a new person. "If anyone is in Christ, he is a new creation. The old has passed away, behold the new has come" (2 Corinthians 5:17). We look, act, and love differently, and that change is a powerful witness to an unbelieving world. A transformed life stands out, because it differs from the way others live. I want to sow seeds everywhere I go and with everyone

I meet, remembering that there are many ways we do that.

One of the things I learned about Natalie through our kitchen talks was that her family owned a section of a rice field that she had worked in all her life. Every season they grow enough rice to feed their family for a year. Three times a year, when the crop comes in, they have to cut the stalks down, bind them into small piles, and then run them through a machine that separates the rice kernel from the shaft. It's a long process and it is very, very hard work. Especially with the sun beating down on your back. On a typical day during harvest time, Natalie gets up at 5 a.m., cooks rice and fish for her family, washes the family's clothes by hand, hangs them out to dry, cleans her house, and then arrives at my door between 8:00 and 8:30.

After she would clean my house, finishing around 2 p.m., she would eat lunch, rest a little, and then, in the heat of the day, head to the rice field until 6-ish.

The green of the rice fields is incredible when the rice is in bloom— absolutely spectacular. I loved to watch people work in the fields. There is something about the dark, wrinkled faces, bodies hunched over under rice hats, that made my heart swell. So I asked Natalie if I could work alongside her for one day.

"Oh it's so dirty! It's so wet! You won't like it," she told me.

"Yes I will. I *want* to…"

"Oh it's too hot, isn't it?" she asked.

"I can do it. I *want* to work there with you."

She got in one last "are you sure?" before I was able to end the back-and-forthing with a definitive "I'm sure."

When the day arrived, I could not have been more excited, or anxious. I put on a pair of hospital scrub pants, an old T-shirt, tucked my hair away, and grabbed a water bottle. Natalie's entire village was out in the fields, all working to provide food for their families. I smiled as I passed the throngs of people staring, and I do mean staring. It's not every day that a white lady comes to work in the rice fields.

I put on my brand-new rice field hat, which I had bought months earlier intending it to be a souvenir. I put on some borrowed rubber boots and stepped into the fields like I had been doing this all my life. My initial observation was that it was *really* muddy. So much so that our boots got stuck and we couldn't lift our feet!

Natalie and I started cracking up, and I consoled myself with the fact that Natalie's feet were stuck as well. Once she got hers free she just took her boots off, laid them aside, and went in barefoot. No big deal, right? But when I tried to do the same, I fell twice. Both times I went down flat on my booty in muddy water. It really was hilarious and neither one of us could help but laugh. Finally I got the boots off and gave myself a pep talk. "Who cares about the bugs and who knows what else that's lurking in that muddy water? I want to do it the way she does." I got right back in, barefoot.

Compared to the other workers, I looked and acted like a klutz. Despite what I wanted to communicate, I had no idea what I was doing. I grabbed the machete that Natalie had provided, put on the gloves she insisted that I wear, got a quick demonstration from her, and then started cutting. It was awesome. And every person who walked past me (there were several) said, "Oh you're so good at that."

Except for one painfully honest person who let me know I was holding the shafts of the rice plants upside down! Once I righted that and got the hang of it all, I was loving it. Natalie and I worked and chatted, having a blast. Although I think Natalie still couldn't believe she was seeing her "boss" working in the rice fields, she was absolutely beaming. I could tell that although she loved having me with her, she was also a little worried about me. She continually brought out cups of water, along with cut-up watermelon and bananas. I asked if she always brought a snack along.

"Oh yes," she said.

Hmm…yeah right. She would never want me to think this was a first. Even in the muddy rice fields standing in our bare feet, I was still her honored guest and she wanted to take care of me.

The next day I couldn't wait to get back to the fields, and this time I brought Jordan along. Now we were really the talk of Natalie's village. Jordan had developed a heart for farming and agriculture during our time in Southeast Asia through volunteer work that he did. Natalie was thrilled to have him there. Her teenage son also came to work alongside us, or maybe just to see for himself the unusual sight of white people working such a dirty job. At one point he and Jordan took off on a motorbike to get fresh coconuts for us to drink and eat. Natalie's son shimmied himself up a tree to grab four or five coconuts, and soon they were back. Taking a break together, drinking from fresh coconuts and relaxing from the hard but super fun work, was definitely a "I love my life" moment for me. I was so proud of Jordan, who loved helping with whatever they needed him to do. As we gathered up the hundreds of piles we had cut, he said, "Mom, this is their food. I don't want to drop any of it, not even one stalk."

There is something incredibly powerful and humbling about knowing that what we were doing was going to help feed this precious family for a year. Life was so uncertain there that they knew, should sickness or job loss come, they would at least be able to live off the rice they had grown. They would have food, and that would be enough. The rice wasn't just their sustenance, it was their security.

Working in rice fields with my dear Natalie was one of the experiences I will hold in my heart for the rest of my life. At one point she said, "I will feel so sad next year when I do this and you aren't here. I will remember that we did this together."

I told her to stop, my heart couldn't take it. And when our work for the day was finished, as Curt drove us all back to her house, I told her to sleep well after all that hard work. And Natalie, whose sleep depends on the state of her heart, said, "Oh yes, I will sleep very well tonight because I am so happy."

Chapter 24

GOD USES DREAMS AND VISIONS

The Recasting of a New Testament Story in a Dream

Dreams and visions are serious business in Southeast Asia. In the West, nighttime dreams are something most people experience but do not give much weight to. We may tell a friend or family member: "Man, I had the weirdest dream last night." Or we might shudder upon awakening after having a nightmare that seemed far too real. But even then, it is quickly forgotten amid the day's events. But in the East, especially for Muslims, dreams and visions can be life-changing.

I'd take them seriously, too, if I had the kind of dreams they do. My Muslim friends had dreams that were crystal clear and very spiritual. In a dream they sometimes see Isa (the Arabic name for Jesus). When I heard about this, I realized I would love to have that type of dream.

One evening I was talking with Adele, a devout Muslim woman about my age. She had been studying the Bible for years. (It was given to her by another Western friend.) Although technically Islam permits Muslims to read the New Testament, in our strict province it was something that people kept hidden. If your curiosity or spiritual hunger drove you to read the Bible, you didn't tell others about it.

Shortly after the tsunami, Adele came to the understanding that Jesus was the Son of God and that He had died to save her from the penalty for her sins. She knew that believing in Him was her only hope for eternity, but she had not yet given her life to Him.

Just as she was close to making the life-changing decision to follow Jesus, her mother fell gravely ill. On her death bed, her mother made Adele promise to remain a Muslim. As was the case with Lee and other Muslim friends, honoring your parents' wishes, even above your own, is huge in Islam. Adele promised her mother that she would remain Muslim, and the battle for her soul began to rage. Her heart had been won by Jesus, but her head and the traditions of her culture would not let go. Satan used these influences to hold onto her soul. He would not surrender Adele to faith in Christ without putting up a huge fight.

She asked to come to my house one night so she could tell me about a dream she'd had. "I was standing on a rickety bridge over a body of water and the water was rising," she began. "I could see that the water was parted in two, and down the middle was a straight, smooth road. A car was traveling down that road. Then the car stopped and I was offered a ride, but I was too afraid to get off the bridge and into the car—even though I knew the bridge wasn't secure and the car and the straight road were."

What a clear picture of Matthew 14. Here is how the English Standard Version describes a scene with Jesus and his disciples:

Immediately he made the disciples get into the boat and go before him to the other side, while he dismissed the crowds. And after he had dismissed the crowds, he went up on the mountain by himself to pray. When evening came, he was there alone, but the boat by this time was a long way from the land, beaten by the waves, for the wind was against them. And in the fourth watch of the night he came to them, walking on the sea. But when the disciples saw him walking on the sea, they were terrified, and said, "It is a ghost!" and they cried out in fear. But immediately Jesus spoke to them, saying, "Take heart; it is I. Do not be afraid."

And Peter answered him, "Lord, if it is you, command me to come to you on the water." He said, "Come." So Peter got out of the boat and walked on the water and came to Jesus. But when he saw the wind, he was afraid, and beginning to sink he cried out, "Lord, save me." Jesus immediately reached out his hand and took hold of him, saying to him, "O you of little faith, why did you doubt?" And when they got into the boat, the wind ceased. And those in the boat worshiped him, saying, "Truly you are the Son of God." (Matthew 14:22–32)

I was so stunned at the clarity of Adele's dream and what the Lord was trying to say to her that it took me a minute to compose myself. I told her that I believed she was like Peter, wanting to believe and yet very afraid. I told her that the car and the "straight and smooth road" represented Jesus. That He was the way out, the safe haven for her, the One who would take her down the "straight path" that Muslims ask God to show them. And with this invitation from Jesus, she had to make the decision to get into the car herself. She had to step off the bridge and into the car if she wanted to get on the straight path she had prayed for all her life.

I also reminded her to of Mark 9:24: "Immediately the father of the child cried out and said, I believe; help my unbelief!" Sometimes faith requires us to step off a cliff and trust that we will be caught.

I know what a huge obstacle it is to let go of the only way you have ever known, a cultural stronghold, a decision that would go against your mother's dying request. Having been raised in the Catholic culture by a mother who strongly followed the Catholic church all of her life, I wasn't asking Adele to do anything that I hadn't done myself. Although the consequences to her would be far greater. At the very least she would be disowned by her family and banished from her village. And if she were to publicly profess Christ as Lord, she could be beaten and face criminal prosecution under Shari'a law for leaving the Muslim faith.

I pray for the day when Adele will overcome her unbelief and step off the rickety bridge and into the safe car traveling down the straight and narrow path.

Chapter 25

RUN FOR YOUR LIFE

A Real-Life Picture of Why It's So Hard to Turn Away from a Lie

When we have a natural disaster in America, we have plenty of resources to care for the injured, to clean up the destruction, and to rebuild communities. But in Southeast Asia, Curt and I and other members of our team were entering an area where hundreds of thousands of lives had been lost and entire villages had disappeared. Those who were left behind were, in many cases, injured, sick, homeless, and grieving over having lost their families. Livelihoods had been washed away. It's hard to imagine the after-effects of the tsunami unless you go there to work among the survivors.

Still, we were not prepared for just how raw the people's emotions would be.

We all have known fear to some degree. Once when we were trying to get on a crowded subway train in Paris, the doors began to close after Curt had boarded. But Molly and I were in the doorway and Jordan was still on the platform. Fear. Panic. Adrenaline. Terror.

And then there is mass panic, which transcends the fears we have as individuals. Probably the only time anyone in my family experienced mass panic was as we watched the events in New York City unfold on September 11, 2001. Even then, seeing the wrenching events on television was a far cry from what people were experiencing at the World Trade Center, the Pentagon, and on United flight 93, which crashed in Pennsylvania.

But in Southeast Asia, Curt witnessed something that gave us a strong hint of what our neighbors had gone through and why the effects of the natural disaster still colored their lives. Curt had been preparing for the annual meeting of a brick factory co-operative that he consulted with. The co-op was based in a rural district that had been devastated by the tsunami. Try to picture the unreal setting. You drive down dirt roads into a jungle where thatch-roofed structures sit in small clearings, surrounded by banana trees. It is serene and spectacular, like something out of a movie or exotic photos you'd see in a travel magazine.

The brick co-op had been instrumental in breathing life back into the economy of this district, and the business was at a crossroads. After two years of essentially being led by Westerners, the members could now begin to take over the leadership. Curt was helping to facilitate a smooth transition.

Having arrived a bit early, he was sitting in his car looking over financial reports. The office was locked and he was waiting for his colleagues to arrive. It was hot and still in the middle of this dense jungle. Then, with his nose buried in profit/loss statements and sweat beginning to run down his back, he realized the atmosphere had suddenly changed.

Curt saw a solitary figure running down a dirt road, coming toward him. The man kept glancing over his shoulder as he ran. Curt said the look of fear on the man's face was intense. Within seconds, the

first man was followed by other men, women carrying babies, children, and motorbikes carrying as many as four people each. Every face
was twisted in fear and the escaping people kept casting glances back
toward where they had come from.

Where were they going? What should he do? Curt realized that if
the locals were running to escape something, then he should run as
well. Either a tsunami was coming or, because this province had re-
cently ended a long-running civil war, perhaps the rebels had obtained
replacement weapons and were once again engaging government
forces in battle.

But neither scenario made sense. Earthquakes precede a tsunami
and Curt hadn't felt a quake that morning. At the same time, the
peace agreement had just had its two-year anniversary and seemed to
be holding. So he remained in his car, sweating and trying to make
sense of the terror shown in the eyes of the people running past.

He reached for his cell phone and called me at home. Jordan answered and Curt asked him: "Did you feel an earthquake this
morning?"

Jordan said he hadn't and then handed me the phone. Curt described the scene in the jungle. His voice revealed the strain he was
under. He said he needed to find out what was happening, fast, and
then he hung up. He saw two locals that he knew and shouted to them
as they rode past on motorbikes. One didn't hear him but the other
did. The man shouted one word in response. "Run!"

One thing we had learned about cross-cultural living was that
when the locals tell you to do something, you do it (within reason). So
Curt started the car and began to drive, not knowing what he was
avoiding or where he should go. He followed the direction of the locals
because they clearly knew something he didn't. The single-lane road
was packed with motorbikes and people and the scene was absolute

pandemonium. Families, old people, and children were running and slipping in the mud. He came up behind a line of dump trucks filled with people, and even more people were trying to scale the sides to get on board. A man on a motorbike pulled alongside Curt. The man shouted, "Can you take my mother and my sister?"

"Sure," Curt nodded. Then he asked: "Where?"

"Away!" The man's voice was urgent as he drove off.

The two women climbed into the back seat of Curt's car. The young girl was sobbing and the old woman was talking rapidly in the local dialect. Using the national language, Curt asked what was going on. The girl continued to sob and the woman failed to answer Curt's question.

Ahead of the car, a mass of people dashed through mud, with motorbikes darting in between pedestrians and cars. Mud was drenching everyone. Curt couldn't afford to take his eyes off of the scene in front of him, but he felt desperate to know what was going on. He had never before had firsthand experience with mass panic.

He grabbed his phone and called a co-worker. There had been no earthquake, he was told. Curt asked our friend to talk with the people in his car while he drove. He practically threw the phone into the back seat and pushed ahead admid the chaos. Soon a woman was clawing at the passenger window pleading to get in the car. As Curt fumbled for the phone, which the old woman in the back seat had returned to him, he tried to unlock the door. The woman outside was shrieking in panic but Curt couldn't get the door unlocked with her pulling up on the handle.

"Wait a moment!" he shouted, and she finally relented. Covered in mud, she lurched inside the car.

Curt started talking to his friend on the phone. The man explained that the woman and the girl in the back seat had heard there was a tsunami and wanted to head to the mountains. He said that, to his knowledge, there hadn't been an earthquake. Curt hung up and, as calmly as he could, began repeating, "There wasn't an earthquake, so there isn't a tsunami."

Fearing that someone would fall under the car in the panic and realizing that he had no idea where he was headed, Curt looked for a place to stop. Spotting an open field, he pulled the car off the road and parked. Curt calmly told the three passengers again that there was no need to panic and no need to escape. He explained that he could take them back to where he had picked them up, or they could continue on afoot. The three elected to continue without him.

∞

Curt slowly made his way back to the meeting place for the co-op board and workers. On the way he got turned around, so it took another hour before he arrived at the office. It was there that he finally learned what really had happened. A switch at a new tsunami warning tower had malfunctioned and the alarm had sounded. It was a false alarm and it took an hour to shut it off.

The same level of panic had also torn through the city. Our helper, Natalie, and her husband were at the hospital waiting for a doctor appointment when suddenly people began running. Doctors, nurses, and patients all fled, leaving behind those who couldn't walk.

If you wonder why a warning siren would cause such mass terror and chaos, consider that most, if not all, of the people seeking to escape on that muddy road had lost someone in the 2004 tsunami. It was easy for Curt to turn back after receiving confirmation that there had been no earthquake. But the people were absolutely convinced. Their experience…their history…their culture…their fear…told them to run.

Curt could only take them so far that day and then the locals he encountered had to make a choice. Choosing to turn around and go back, when everyone you know is headed in the same (opposite) direction, is something that will not come naturally in this place.

In many ways, Curt's experience that day summed up the spiritual state of this province. Followers of Christ walk in the light of the truth—living it and sharing it. Yet the chains that bind hearts, close ears, and blind eyes prevent many of the province's residents from turning toward the Truth. Five times a day they respond to another false alarm—one that blares from loudspeakers in every neighborhood and leads them away from the Truth. History, culture, and fear tell them to keep going…in the wrong direction.

Chapter 26

ATTRACTING NEGATIVE ATTENTION

We Are Responsible to Protect Our Hearts

My daughter, Molly, was only eleven when we moved to Southeast Asia. Having grown up in North Carolina, she had the security of a very protective father and older brother. Molly knew what it meant to be honored, and she had a deep sense of her worth and value as a young woman. Every moment of her life, the two most important men in her world loved and nurtured her so very well.

She had been told all her life that she was beautiful inside and out, and that someday a godly man would realize she was well worth waiting for. She knew that until the day she was married, her father and her brother were the guardians of her heart. She had always been treated with respect by the men in her life, including her grandfather, uncle, and friends of our family.

That was back in North Carolina. We quickly realized that living in a strict Muslim province in Southeast Asia we faced a different set of challenges. In many areas of the world, Western women are viewed as promiscuous because of the images portrayed on television, in movies, and in other forms of American entertainment that finds its way overseas.

Before we left the States, I read a painfully honest account of an American woman who grew up in a Muslim country. She described how the stares, leers, and even gropes of Muslim men had deeply affected her heart. As parents we must take our daughters' feelings and experiences seriously. And we must be wise about the advice we give them.

In any culture that actively devalues women, telling your daughter to "just ignore" the stares, comments, and touching is one of the worst things you can do. It dismisses her legitimate feelings of embarrassment, shame, and violation. It also is wrong to explain away the violating behaviors by saying that "these people are lost so they can't help it." A misguided turn-the-other-cheek response will not protect your daughter's heart.

Having read the account of the woman who carried emotional scars from having lived in a Muslim culture, I knew I had to discuss these things with my family. Before we left the States, we talked about how each of us had to be vigilant to protect Molly, physically and emotionally. I felt we were going into it with our eyes open, but once we moved I could see we were not prepared for just how difficult it would be.

On the first full day in our new city, we went to the market with a local family. This was a vast, outdoor, tarp-and-tin-roof-covered area where clothing, housewares, fabrics, fruit, vegetables, and other items were sold. It wasn't a dressed-up, touristy market, but the place where locals went to buy what they needed.

As we tried to navigate the noisy, narrow, claustrophobic aisles of the market, I saw an older man's face light up as Molly approached. Then he reached his hands out to try to touch her, even though she was dressed in a culturally appropriate, very modest manner. Horrified, I stood in the gap between my daughter and this man as we quickly passed by. Molly never saw what was happening, and I'm thankful for that. I knew God was showing me from day one that we had to protect her like never before. In this culture, said to be a strict Muslim region, men tend to hold women and even girls in low regard. I didn't see much cultural protection or respect for females, so we knew we had to do the protecting ourselves.

Another time we were in the same market when a young man reached out and touched Molly's arm with a book he was holding. That may seem harmless, but I could tell he meant more by it than just incidental contact. The look in his eyes carried more than mere curiosity about a white foreigner. I turned and looked at him and said, in the harshest tone I could manage: "Don't *ever* touch my daughter, even with a book!"

It would have been culturally appropriate for him to feel ashamed and to heed what an older woman was saying to him, but he just laughed. Unlike the previous experience, this time Molly heard and saw everything. As a result, she ended up hating to go to the market. From that day on, I took her along only if Curt and Jordan went with us. And when we went shopping with them along, you would think they were in the Secret Service the way they guarded us. We learned that the stares and comments weren't as bold when men were walking beside us.

Despite the fact that we were fully covered whenever we went out, we were still Western, white women so we couldn't go anywhere without being stared at. People sometimes would come out of stores, trying to move closer to get a better look. Understand this was not just immature boys checking out a beautiful white girl dressed like a Muslim. It was men of all ages, something we would never tolerate back home.

When the men checked me out I could laugh it off, especially since I felt like I could probably beat up a lot of them. But leering at my daughter? This was something I would not tolerate. The hypocrisy of their behavior was almost enough to make me shout: "You claim to be so holy and devout and yet you leer at a young girl?"

One day Molly and I went shopping to find a red shirt to wear to our team Christmas party. We didn't want to shop in the traditional market so we headed on foot to a retail area near where we lived. As we walked from store to store, and as we rode local transportation, I could feel the stares from men everywhere.

At one point, as we were riding in a sidecar attached to a motorcycle, which was a commonly used form of transportation, I asked Molly to cover her face with her head scarf because a truck full of young men was ahead of us. They had all turned to stare and point at her. (Though the people in our province were for the most part very friendly, hospitable, and kind to us, they just are not discreet when they stare.) I couldn't bear seeing these young men leering at my daughter. She didn't mind covering her face, it helped keep dirt out of our eyes as we rode along.

Although the male Muslim friends that Curt and I made in Southeast Asia were polite and respectful toward me and Molly, it was uncomfortable that so many men would tell us, "You look so beautiful in your head scarf" (yeah right!). I was in my mid-forties, so I could blow these kinds of things off easily. But all of this attention was new to my precious daughter. She didn't want to be told that she is beautiful by a man other than her brother or father.

And though it made me crazy, Jordan was ready to take someone out every time they stared at Molly or said how beautiful she was. I loved seeing him develop such protective instincts over his sister, and I love that that made her feel safe. She knew no one would be able to get past her brother or her father.

The saddest thing was that in many ways, I felt the culture in that Southeast Asian city was safer than America. We didn't have to worry about crime. Child abduction was unheard of in our province, so my kids could walk freely in stores and other public places apart from me. But my daughter never could go anywhere alone. Our biggest fear, for very good reasons, was that a man would touch her. We were careful to make sure that she was never in a position for that to happen.

I saw Molly's personality begin to change from a vibrant, extroverted person who would light up any room to a much more guarded, cautious, careful person who didn't like to attract attention—even good attention. Toward the end of our time in Southeast Asia, I noticed that when we went out, she would walk with her head down. I wanted to protect her heart and keep her safe before all that she had experienced ever had a chance to sink in. Molly wasn't a little girl anymore. She was quickly becoming a beautiful young woman. She was marriage age in Southeast Asian culture.

Maybe it was a good thing that our contract was nearing its end and we could see our work there coming to a close.

Chapter 27

YOU CAN'T OUT-GIVE GOD

A Life That God Blesses and Multiplies

Think about how crazy generous the gospel is—God's making it possible to call us His own. The natural response is gratitude and worship. In the year leading up to our leaving the States, our pastor, J. D. Greear, often taught about the gospel response of generosity. One of his challenges resonated deep in my soul, especially given what we were preparing to do.

"You can't out-give God," J. D. said.

I have to admit that when I heard him say that, my first thought was "I sure hope you're right!"

We were in the letting-go process when we started considering God's generosity to us, and the response of generosity on our part. Curt and I were in our forties, and we were selling off our American life. Most of our friends were focused on financial security and doing what it takes to secure a comfortable retirement.

At first it felt like we were giving up a lot. We seemed to be giving so much to God that He couldn't possibly give us back more than that. If you are giving Him *everything* you have, what is left after that?

While we were living in Southeast Asia, I began reading *Hudson Taylor's Spiritual Secret*. In talking about his decision to step out in faith, Hudson Taylor wrote: "I never made a sacrifice." The compensations were so real and lasting that he came to see that giving is inevitably receiving, if you are dealing heart-to-heart with God. And now, after giving up our upper-middle-class life in North Carolina and living in Southeast Asia, I agree with Hudson Taylor.

After selling just about everything we had, I now say, "so what." I have never missed any of it. When I consider the amount of time and money I spent assembling and maintaining just the right combination of home, furniture, interior decorating, accents, and special touches, I think, *what a waste!*

In Southeast Asia I got to live in a beautiful house that someone else had sacrificially given money to pay the rent on. We had incredible views of pristine mountains covered with trees bearing bananas, mangos, and papayas. Growing all around me were hot peppers, tomatoes, watermelons, and who knows what else. Sure we had ants and lizards, a leaking roof and windows, unreliable electrical service, and no dishwasher or dryer. But every day I was in awe that I got to live on a spectacular tropical island. That still blows my mind. What an honor and privilege. What a gift.

I had never felt that way before about any place I had lived, despite all the comforts I'd enjoyed throughout life. I have owned five homes in the States, and our home in a city in a hot, humid Third World province was my favorite.

After we had been in Southeast Asia for a few months, I found an eight-year-old picture of Curt on the job back at SAS. I put it alongside a picture of him working in the Third World. Though he was eight years younger in the picture taken in America, he looked ten years older. Not only did he appear thinner, younger looking, and happier in the picture taken in the Third World, his new job enabled us to be together more than we were apart. And he had a job that really mattered, for what it did for others, for eternity. He was working to point others to riches far greater than earthly wealth.

We gave up vacations to Hawaii, Europe, and the North Carolina beaches. Instead, we got to see the world.

We moved to where it was always summer, twenty minutes from the most beautiful beach I'd ever seen. During our time in Southeast Asia, receiving by far the lowest salary we'd made during our married years, we travelled to Bali, Singapore, Thailand, and New Zealand. Our kids became experts at navigating airports, immigration lines, and jet lag.

We left a town that had great schools. Instead, my kids got an education they never could have received in any school.

The best school Jordan and Molly ever attended was in their own home, which happened to be in the Third World. When they started homeschooling I saw them rediscover a passion for learning that they had lost when they were in public school. They used a DVD-based curriculum from an accredited school in the States. They read really great books, one after another, that volunteers brought from America or that they found on our teammates' bookshelves. Rather than focusing on getting the necessary score to earn a certain grade to get a high-enough class rank to get into a certain college, they were free to learn for the joy of learning.

In addition, they spent their free time around incredibly well-educated people who had left behind "promising" futures in America to give their lives to something a whole lot bigger than themselves. My kids learned how to speak another language fluently and to love people who were completely different from themselves. They learned how to share their faith with someone who had never heard of Jesus Christ, and with people who had a false idea of what Christianity is. What an incredible life education they received.

I saw my daughter chip in when someone on our team needed help, babysitting, preparing expense reports, and finding great joy out of making chocolate banana smoothies for everyone at the guest house. She developed incredible personal discipline when the only means she had of keeping her passion for ballet alive was practicing by herself.

My son taught himself to play guitar by listening to CDs and figuring out the chords. He learned to play so well that he has played in worship bands back in the States. Both my children learned that God gave them gifts to share with others. Our daughter taught ballet to younger American girls living in our country at annual homeschool conferences, and our son became the worship leader for our house church.

Only God could pluck a life like ours out of Chapel Hill, North Carolina, and bring us to such an incredible place on the other side of the world. Only God could provide for us "far more abundantly than all that we ask or think" (Ephesians 3:20). So the next time you think you have given Him a lot, remember: you *can't* out-give God. My family is proof of that.

When Curt and I were in our forties, instead of bearing down and maximizing our income and pursuing wise investments to prepare for the future, we followed God's call to do something that, on the surface, made absolutely no sense. But J. D. was right: you cannot out-give God.

He called our family to

- give Him our house…so He could give us a home.
- give Him our jobs…so He could give us a calling.
- give Him our financial security…so He could teach us that real security is found only in Him.

- give Him our activities...so He could give us passion.
- give Him our relationships...so He could give us family.
- give Him the "great schools" our kids were enrolled in...so He could give our kids a life education not found in any school.
- give Him our kids...so He, the far greater Parent, could break them and then mold them into the man and woman he created them to be.
- give Him our comfort zone...so He could show us that lasting comfort comes from living in the center of His will, not ours.

There wasn't a single area of our lives that we turned over to God where He has not one-upped us. Every time He showed us, no matter how hard you try, you can't out-give Him.

Chapter 28

We Are Sojourners on Earth

When You Come Back, You Are Not the Same Person

Our initial commitment to Southeast Asia was for two years, and it was easy to extend it to three. After we hit the two-year mark, we felt in many ways like we were only just getting started. We weren't even close to returning to America. In fact, "home" for us was starting to feel like Southeast Asia. As Molly put it, "America will always be there waiting for us. I feel like it's a gift to be able to live here right now."

None of us was in a hurry to get back to the States. We were asked to stay permanently in Southeast Asia and Curt and I began exploring that possibility. We looked at our initial decision process, which now seemed so long ago, and started laughing about the things that initially had made us worry. They seemed so silly to us now. And looking at our life in Southeast Asia, our only concern was thinking that we might have turned down such a phenomenal opportunity. What if we had give in to our fears and stayed in America? Giving in to our fears and staying in the States would have been one of the biggest mistakes of our life.

As we considered an extended future in Southeast Asia, Curt was asked to interview for a position at a new nonprofit in North Carolina. It was created by a brilliant guy who has a passion for his community and an even bigger passion for sharing the love of Christ. But he was already the CEO of a large company. He needed a director for the nonprofit, and he had been given Curt's name.

Curt interviewed over the phone and decided that five years earlier, when he had first become involved with community ministry, he would have jumped at the chance to take this on. But now, after living in a strict Muslim area with little to no gospel witness, he knew that God had called him to international church planting. And that was when our pastor, J. D. Greear, called him about leading The Summit Church in that very area.

With our contract up, our teammates leaving for other assignments, our son nearing college age, and our daughter becoming a woman in a culture that was quickly becoming an unhealthy place for her, we knew God was asking us to return to the States. I told Curt that I respected him as the leader of our family, and I would follow in whatever decision he believed was the Lord's. I knew going back was going to wreak havoc on my heart. And yet, I knew that staying would be excruciating when the time came for us to send Jordan to college. No matter what we did, my heart was going to be broken. Then I reminded myself: obedience is not always easy, but obedience is always best.

One of the hardest days of my life was the day we boarded the plane to leave Southeast Asia. I made Curt promise me that I could come back to Southeast Asia to visit, often, and hopefully to live again someday. He did, and truthfully that is what got me on the plane to

America. We had lost nothing by leaving behind our old life and living for three years in Southeast Asia. In fact, we had gained it all by doing only three things:

Trusting in the Lord with *all our heart*

not leaning on our own understanding (which is such a deceiver),

and *acknowledging Him* in all our ways (see Proverbs 3:5–6).

That's our job. And God's part in all of this is guaranteed: "He will direct your paths" (Proverbs 3:6). He did ours, and we will always be changed, as a result.

∞

Even though I have lived most of my life in America, returning to the States after three years in the Third World was surreal and very, very hard. Admittedly, I did not have the best attitude about returning because I didn't want to leave the place and people I loved. Part of the shock was that, until I got back to North Carolina, I didn't realize how much I had changed. Now everything in America felt big and fast. People were, just as Glen had observed, in a hurry. Making the adjustment even harder was my grief over leaving a country, a life, and work that I loved, and people who had become family to me.

If I had anticipated sympathy or understanding, I was wrong. In the eyes of those we returned to, we heard only that it was "great to have you back." Beyond that, they expected us to get busy. It felt like I had been thrown into a river, and since everyone around me knew I could swim I was expected to fight the current and stay above water. But they forgot I had left loved ones on the shore half a world away.

We had changed, but the United States also had changed in our absence. The economic downturn began while we were away, so we came home to closed businesses, friends without jobs, a sluggish real estate market, and high gasoline prices. It was yet another huge adjustment we would have to make as we tried to figure out how to live in America again.

But returning to North Carolina also brought blessing, joy, and some amusing moments. For one thing, everything looked sparkling clean. I felt like I was wearing a new, clear, sharper set of contact lenses. The day after our arrival, I walked into a Wal-Mart and told the friend who was with me: "Wow, this is soooo clean!" I even asked the cashier, "Is this store brand new? It is beautiful!"

The store was six years old. And it was a Wal-Mart, not Tiffany's. Can you tell I was reverse culture shocking?

∞

The most profound realization would come many months later. Although I knew in my heart that adjustments take time, even after eighteen months the States didn't feel like home. At the time it bothered me. I wondered if I had become a person without a home, or at least a person without a sense of home. But later I understood what was happening. I had never really grasped the idea that "this earth is not my home." In fact, I always thought it was a little weird when my Christian brothers and sisters would say that, as if they were confused about their planet of residence.

How can you say the earth is not your home when you have never lived anywhere else?

Now I get it.

"Home" and "belonging" are important concepts and deeply meaningful to all of us. But for a follower of Jesus, they have a different meaning. As hard as I tried to fit in during three years in Southeast Asia, even if I had never left I still would not have been "one of them." My white skin, American accent, and Western worldview would always have gotten in the way. And yet, in coming back to the States, the place I have lived almost all my life, I am no longer at home either.

The three years that I lived overseas changed me in unexpected and permanent ways. The friends I had prior to moving still love me, of course, and they are still involved in my life. But they can't understand why an American would feel displaced living in America. In many ways, Southeast Asia now feels like home, but I know it never can be, even if I were to move back.

I finally understand that I am a sojourner on earth. A sojourner is a temporary resident, someone who "stays for a time in a place." I am a sojourner wherever I live until I get to my real home, which I've read about for decades. My real home is heaven.

I'm slowly learning to live with the longing to be back in Southeast Asia, and with my discomfort with life in America. Not a day has passed where I do not miss everything about our life overseas. I miss seeing God move in Muslim hearts. I miss the locals, the unity that we experienced with our colleagues, the intensity and intimacy of the relationships with friends. And I miss being surrounded by tropical beauty. I miss the food and even the sound of the call to prayer. I miss my Natalie.

My joy in being in the States for the next few years has to do with the stage my family is in. Jordan is a college student, and Molly is seriously pursuing ballet. But ironically, as much as our children are thriving, I struggle with some of the same questions I had before we moved overseas. I wonder if bringing them back to America was actually the best thing for them.

They miss our teammates, our work, their American friends who are still overseas, the food, and our house church. Living in North Carolina doesn't feel quite the same way it used to, and people seem a little different. I know that we seem a little different to those we have returned to, and we are. Every time I wonder about these things, God reminds me: "For I know the plans I have for you…" (Jeremiah 29:11).

In His infinite graciousness, He has continued to provide "far more abundantly than all that we ask or think" (Eph 3:20). He provided Southeast Asian friends for us right in Chapel Hill. They keep my language skills active and my heart beating for my adopted second home. It means the world to me to spend time with them.

One of the hardest things we "gave up" when we left the other side of the world was living with and working alongside the best people we have ever known. But God my Father, the Giver of "every good gift and every perfect gift" (James 1:17), has continued to give us opportunities to be together with them. Our former teammates continue to be stellar examples of what a gospel-centered life looks like. They are incredibly smart, talented people who chose to lay aside a life of physical comfort to pursue eternity.

My children spent formative years surrounded by this group of people, who modeled servanthood, grace, love, integrity, perseverance, and the value and fun of having and keeping a sense of humor. I grieved when we parted, wondering when or how we would be together again. And yet I don't think a month has gone by where we haven't seen at least one of them.

Curt accepted the position of Pastor of Church Planting with The Summit Church in Durham, North Carolina. His overseas experience and maturity were very much needed in this position. We continue to work on seeing the gospel taken to dark places in this world where people have never heard about Jesus. It is an honor to serve alongside those who served and supported us when we really needed it. I don't know how long God will have us remain in the States. I just know that for this season, He has called us to this place. Obedience is definitely hard, but it's ultimately and always so worth it.

Being back in the States has given us a deeper and more accurate perspective on what it means to obey God's call to discipleship. It is not about relieving your boredom, or plunging into an extreme adventure, or joining the latest wave of whatever is being talked about by North American Christians. We are not called to go and be a do-gooder so we can feel better about ourselves. It has nothing to do with you and everything to do with Christ and His Kingdom.

Where we went was a hard, hard place to live. Our work, our relationships, and our strategy were under constant spiritual attack. On the hardest days, when I felt like I had nothing left, I held onto one truth. We were exactly where we were supposed to be, we were exactly where God called us to be...and that was enough.

We didn't go to serve our team, our city, or even the people we grew to absolutely love. While I don't deny that indeed we served all of them, if they were our main reason for being there we would've left before our contract was up. We would have succumbed to the never-ending disappointments, frustrations, and challenges. But instead, we went to Southeast Asia to serve God first and foremost. And He was faithful through every hour of every day. He is at the center of our family's story and will remain there, no matter what side of the world we find ourselves on.

We weren't seeking adventure. We weren't in need of a mid-life shift to something more exciting. We had no desire to do the cool thing. Remember, we thought our life was perfect just the way it was. But we were wrong. We have only one task, and it will be the same today as the day before and the day before that. Just to walk in obedience, following Christ no matter where He leads, without any conditions.

Evangelical theologian Carl F.H. Henry said, "The Gospel is only good news if it gets there in time." For a season in our life the Lord told us, "Go." That is why we went. On the days when I felt empty and useless, God reminded me that He doesn't call the equipped, He equips the called.

We went because God told us to, and because the gospel is absolutely worth it.

Chapter 29

OUR KIDS SPEAK OUT

What Jordan and Molly Think Today about Their Life Overseas

Parents want what is best for their children. We all face decisions about how to handle cultural influences, household rules, our children's friendships, their involvement in school and after-school activities, and ministry involvement. So it's understandable that I am frequently asked how our three years in Southeast Asia affected Molly and Jordan. Perhaps the person asking the question has considered answering God's call to obedience, and is wondering how that could affect his or her family. But more often than not, people are just curious. And when they do ask, usually there is an underlying tone of expectation that some kind of horror story will follow.

The other comment I hear a lot is "that must have been quite an *experience* for them." I have to bite my tongue on that one. It wasn't just an experience, it was three very formative years of their *life*. But no matter the comments or questions, my answer is always the same: "It was the best thing we ever did for them." People don't realize that bringing our kids back to the United States was a bigger struggle than the decision to move our family to Southeast Asia.

When we got back to North Carolina I began to identify some of the greatest gifts my children received by living overseas. They experienced intensive, intentional discipleship, away from the distractions and influences of their home culture. Living and working alongside adults who had planted their lives in difficult places for the sake of the gospel was a powerful example of sacrificial, intentional obedience. Living in a culture where Jordan and Molly were a social, religious, and ethnic minority, stripped of everything that was familiar (except their family and their faith), brought them to the end of themselves. And *that* made all the difference. Allowing God to break my kids is the best thing we ever did for them.

But that's my perspective. Now at age twenty and seventeen, Jordan and Molly are well able to tell their own stories, which I invited them to do.

"I wasn't afraid to move overseas," Jordan reflected. "Because we have moved a lot, I didn't feel very connected at my high school after my freshman year, and I didn't yet have a good group of close friends. I thought moving would be fun and a fresh start. I had never been very content about living in the South anyway. Living overseas would be a unique opportunity that would be something very different from the lives the kids at home had."

Molly felt differently.

"To be honest, I was scared when Dad went to Southeast Asia on that first trip for six weeks. He was going to a strict Muslim area that had just had a deadly tsunami. It was a place I had never heard of, so I didn't know what to expect. That is when I began the practice I have today of reading my Bible every day. It became my source of confidence. I knew my Dad was in God's hands and that God could be fully trusted with someone I love so much. And the photos and emails he sent helped too.

"When it came time for our family to move, I wasn't afraid. I knew my dad wouldn't take me somewhere unsafe. It helped to know that he had gone before us. So I was excited about the adventure of living on a tropical island with palm trees everywhere, of learning to speak a new language, and learning about a new culture."

Both Jordan and Molly faced culture shock when we arrived in our new country. Molly recalled two moments when it hit her the hardest.

"Getting off that excruciatingly long plane ride, standing in line for immigration, feeling so jet lagged, exhausted, and hot, was my first taste of culture shock. Everything looked, sounded, smelled, and felt *so* different. And then when we used the airport bathroom and saw the squatty potty and there was water all over the floor, I thought, *Whoa*. The capital city where we stayed for the first few days was not at all like the pictures dad had showed us. It was a mega-city. I didn't see many palm trees.

"My second taste of culture shock happened soon after we arrived in the province where we would be living. We went in to the local marketplace. It was so cramped and I had never felt so uncomfortably hot before, with my head scarf and long sleeves on. The animals roaming around, the open sewers, the language, it was so radically different than our clean, orderly America."

Jordan had a different experience. His culture shock was more gradual and eventually caught up with him.

"I learned how to persevere through trials in Southeast Asia," he now says. "Reading and meditating deeply on the Book of James is what got me through my culture shock. 'Count it all joy my brothers, when you meet trials of various kinds, for you know that the testing of your faith produces steadfastness' (James 1:2–3). Additionally, reading The Heavenly Man, about a severely persecuted and courageous house church leader in China, and Bruchko, about a nineteen-year old American who suffered greatly for the gospel, gave me a different perspective on my own 'trials'—which in comparison didn't seem like trials at all."

Although it may be years before they realize the full extent of all that they learned overseas, Jordan and Molly already know they learned valuable life lessons.

"I learned, saw, and lived out what it means to be a true follower of Christ and not just a cultural Christian," Jordan said. "You couldn't afford to be just a cultural Christian and survive where we lived. Although this was a great perspective to gain at a young age, it made attending a Christian university back in the States difficult for me. That has been the hardest thing about being back. The prevalence of cultural Christianity in America has been a challenge.

"Living in such a radically different country and culture, I had to rely on other believers in a way that we don't have to in the States. We literally had to say to each other, 'I need you, I need your help.' The sense of community we had was so strong because we were all that we had. One of my best memories is our house church. I loved how we had to *participate* in church, rather than consume it. It was awesome to get into the Word together without any distractions. I really learned to love group discussion as a result of being in a house church."

Molly too loved the strong sense of community.

"I saw and experienced a body of believers living and working together in community. I loved the shared vision we had. You couldn't be independent or you wouldn't survive. I saw how valuable partnership in ministry is. It made me realize that I wouldn't want to go overseas as an unmarried person because partnership is too important to me now. I love the true sense of fellowship that I experienced on our team."

Living in a strict Muslim province also changed Jordan and Molly's perspective on Islam and its followers.

Jordan recalled, "Prior to moving to Southeast Asia, I had a 9/11 perception of Muslims. But after living alongside them, getting to know them and sharing life together, I learned that they are people in desperate need of the gospel, just like anyone else."

Molly said, "After seeing their works-based religion lived out in front of me, it made me thankful for the freedom I have as a follower of Christ."

There were many simple lessons they learned from daily life as well.

"I learned how to be flexible with my time and my schedule, because there weren't any schedules that we had to follow," Jordan said. "There were times where we got an invitation to a wedding fifteen minutes before it was to start, so we learned to make people and relationships a priority rather than what we were busying ourselves with at the moment.

"Before I moved overseas I was somewhat of a picky eater. But I learned the importance of contextualization in building successful cross-cultural relationships. So I learned to love their very different and very spicy food. I absolutely prefer international cuisine now. I also grew to enjoy wearing some of the cultural clothing. I wanted to show my local friends that I cared about them by being willing to step out of my own comfort zone and be a part of their culture. I couldn't have a typical American teenage mindset of 'sorry, but that's just not my thing.'

"I learned about real hospitality and true community from the people we lived and worked with. I felt so deeply connected to the people there. I miss that strong sense of community that is very hard to duplicate here in the States."

Molly too confessed that one of the hardest parts about being back in the States was losing the strong sense of community.

"I know that living there was special," she told me, tears in her eyes. "It was a gift. Once I got used to the inconveniences I learned to love the simplicity of life there. We had a very laid-back lifestyle. We considered a 'good day' one in which we had uninterrupted electricity all day and night. I also loved having my dad with us as much as he was. I loved riding my bike to the rice fields and talking to Natalie every day.

"One of my favorite memories was riding my bike alongside Natalie as she went to the tiny market in her village to buy fresh vegetables every day. I loved that we could walk home with Natalie and step into a traditional village right next to our neighborhood. I loved seeing how she and her relatives lived. Her village was its own little world to me. Sometimes the people in her village would be without running water, and none of them had any modern conveniences or appliances. There were chickens, goats, and ducks roaming around everywhere and yet the people were perfectly content and happy."

Living as the only Christians in a strict Muslim area, both Jordan and Molly learned valuable lessons about their faith.

"I learned how to be very certain about my beliefs," said Jordan. "When I had an unforgettable conversation with my friend Usher, in which he asked if I thought he was going to go to heaven when he died, I had a decision to make. Was it more compassionate to give him the answer he wanted to hear, or was it more loving to tell him the Truth? I realized in that moment that if universalism were true, then what we had done over those three years was in vain. I told Usher the Truth."

Molly learned to value the Word and how to trust God in a way that I think has made her very different from her peers.

"I learned how to hunger for God's Word because I wasn't going to church where I could just sit and listen to a sermon. I learned so much by reading the Bible intensively," she said. "I love the Bible that I used there because it's full of highlighted passages and notes that I took. I knew I had to know the Word well if I was going to be protected from Satan's attacks in a very dark place.

"I also learned that God takes care of everything, from big deals to small details. I certainly saw that in the way He provided for my ballet. Only He could have done that. But I also learned that He takes care of things only one step at a time. He took care of me and He erased all my fears, but He did it one day at a time. It was definitely a process.

"Now that I am seventeen, I don't value popularity or being cool as my peers do. When you live in a culture that is so radically different, you learn how to give your fears over to God, because He is your only constant. I think that is what made me find my identity in Christ and my security in Him, because I was taken away from everything except for my parents, my brother, and Him. God showed me who I am in Christ, not who I am in the eyes of peers or friends. If I didn't have this life experience of living overseas, I probably would be struggling with the same insecurities that other teenage girls do."

After two years back in the States, with Jordan in his second year of college and Molly in her last two years of high school, I asked them to reflect on how they had changed. Their responses were quite similar.

"Now that I am home," said Jordan, "I realize that I am not 100% Western anymore. Spending the first fifteen years of my life in America is very significant and I can't deny that part of my life. I am thankful to be part of a unique community of people who spent part of their formative years growing up in another culture. I wouldn't trade where

I have grown up, in America and Southeast Asia, for anything.

"My family was close before we moved overseas. But in Southeast Asia, we were together 24/7 and we grew even closer, especially my sister and me. We became each other's best friend. Before we moved overseas, the rest of the world was sadly not really on my radar. I was focused on what was going on in the States and that was it. And now, my future is certainly not limited to living and working in America. I find that news sources are more relevant and interesting to me if they have an international focus. Although I do care about what is going on in America, the famine in Somalia is more important to me than our nation's debt crisis. There is so much more that is happening in the world than what is going on in our own back yard. Living overseas gave me a global perspective.

"Unlike many of my peers, through direct experience I have lived more than just white, middle-class suburbia. I know that life really is not all about me. If I really believe the Bible and I go to a place that is hostile to the gospel, what do I have to lose? I have seen this firsthand, and either way I die in the end. The luxuries of this life are temporary. The most important task is taking the gospel to where it is not yet known. Christianity calls us to something so much greater than just Sunday services and living a moral life.

"Since I am attending college in Alabama, I have the privilege of being able to attend The Church at Brook Hills where Dr. David Platt is the lead pastor. Sitting under his weekly teaching and reading his book Radical has challenged me to contemplate even more the absolute claims of the gospel and how it calls us to say, 'Here is my life God. I'm putting it on the table. Take it. It's yours.'

"I have a strong sense of thankfulness for having lived in Southeast Asia. It wasn't easy, but I would absolutely do it all again."

And finally, Molly: "I realized that not everyone in the world wants to be American or live in America. The world is so much bigger than our fifty states. I felt so disconnected from America while we were away, and that turned out not to be a bad thing. I bonded with my new culture because I was able to be fully there. I didn't have satellite TV and I didn't use the Internet very much, so I was not distracted by what was happening on the other side of the world in America.

"One of the biggest things I learned was the value of my sibling. He's the partner in life that God has given to me while I am growing up and until each one of us gets married. Most of my peers find their BFF outside of their immediate family. But I have never known life without my brother, and he is the only other person in the world who has been through what I have. It's sad to me how many siblings are not close. My brother and I may have eventually become distant had we stayed in the States, especially if we were at different schools and had different friends. But my brother went to high school and I went to middle school in the same room for three years in our house in Southeast Asia. We were all each other had, and we wouldn't have wanted it any other way.

"As the youngest in our family, I am always in a position of looking up. In Southeast Asia I got to see firsthand what a strong leader my dad is for our family. My mom, who is a people person to the nth degree, got our family out of our house and into relationships. My brother knows the Word better than anyone I know. I learned so much watching my family learn to live in Southeast Asia. Apart from the Lord, only the four of us really know the transformation that happened there. Because we went through it *together*."

Chapter 30

WHAT COMPELS US

Our Greatest Treasure Is in the Gospel

No matter what side of the world we find ourselves on, there will always be one thing that compels our family to do what we do. We found this to be the most valuable pursuit in life, because it has the most satisfying rewards and gives us the greatest return on our investment. It is the gospel.

The gospel is not a style of music—"black ladies singing in church"—as my lifelong friend and adopted brother Jimmy mistakenly thought. The gospel is, as my pastor says, "that you and I are more wicked than we ever dreamed, and God is more loving and merciful than you and I ever deserved." And that isn't J. D.'s or even Hilary Alan's opinion, that is what the Bible tells us.

Sadly, the gospel is getting largely dismissed by our culture, which is so uber saturated with postmodern thought. People tend to live with an "I believe, therefore it is" approach. But the Bible shares very little in common with the preferences of North American culture. In stark contrast, the scriptures confront us with something that is very different, very radical, and these days, very unpopular: "For all have sinned and fall short of the glory of God" (Romans 3:23). And "No one is righteous, no, not one" (Romans 3:10).

That means everyone is born a sinner. It is our human condition. Every time we act or think apart from what is God's best for us, we sin, which is offensive to a holy God. That means every time we are impatient, rude, selfish, think an unkind thought, or think only of ourselves, we sin. And because humans are the way they are, this means that every human sins every day, many times. And this sin separates us from God because He is holy, and we are not. That's not good news for any of us.

Human nature also drives us to want to be in control, and to believe that we are. This extends to thinking we can control what happens beyond the grave.

You see evidence of this when someone says, "If I am a good person I will go to heaven when I die. Everyone does bad things, because none of us is perfect. But at least I never killed anyone or did anything really bad. God will forgive me. He knows my heart."

Yes, he does! And our hearts are by nature, wicked. Because God is holy, his standard is one hundred percent holiness, a standard that none of us can meet. Unlike every other religion that teaches "Do this and you will attain salvation," Christianity is the only "religion" that teaches "what you could never do on your own, Christ did for you." It is impossible for us to meet God's standard of complete holiness.

But it doesn't stop there. God says we all will stand in judgment to give an account of our lives. And since we all have sinned, we deserve punishment. "For the wages of sin is death" (Romans 6:23).

And that is the reason Jesus Christ came to earth. He came to live the life that you and I were supposed to live, a sinless life, and to die the death that you and I deserve, because we are sinners. There is good news on the other side of the verse I just quoted: "but the free gift of

God is eternal life in Christ Jesus our Lord" (Romans 6:23).

Instead of the death that we deserve, Jesus came to die in our place, so we could be restored to God. "Jesus said to him, I am the way and the truth and the life. No one comes to the Father except through me" (John 14:6).

This is where the Gospel gets really unpopular. Because we want to do things our way. But the Bible is very clear: the only way to God is through Jesus! So how do we get the free gift that God has offered to everyone?

"If you confess with your mouth Jesus is Lord and believe in your heart that God raised Him from the dead, you will be saved" (Romans 10:9). "For everyone who calls on the name of the Lord will be saved" (Romans 10:13).

That is the gospel. I didn't hear the gospel until I was in my early twenties. Though I had grown up in the Catholic Church, I never met Jesus there. I was taken to mass every Sunday by my mother, memorized all the ritual prayers, and completed all the sacraments of the church while never understanding what any of it meant.

The first person I ever saw reading a Bible was my husband. Shortly after I met him, I opened a Bible on my own and read John 14:1-6 for the first time.

Let not your hearts be troubled. Believe in God, believe also in me. In my Father's house are many rooms. If it were not so, would I have told you that I go to prepare a place for you? And if I go and prepare a place for you, I will come again and will take you to myself, that where I am you may be also. And you know the way to where I am going. Thomas said to him, 'Lord we do not know where you are going. How can we know the way?' Jesus said to him, 'I am the way and the truth and the life. No one comes to the Father except through me. (John 14:1–6)

Whoa, Jesus is real? were my immediate thoughts.

I met Jesus that night. Over the next several years I spent hours asking Curt endless questions about Jesus and what it meant to be a Christian. He was so patient with me. I read the Bible cover to cover, over and over, and couldn't believe all that was in there and all that I had been missing out on because no one had told me the Truth!

But despite what I wanted to think, I was still living for myself. I was relying on Curt's and my ability to make a good living, to make wise decisions, to give our family all the advantages. Even though I was reading the Bible and on a quest to know God, money and comfort were my functional gods.

Then in 1999, due to a personal financial crisis, we finally put Jesus in His rightful place and let Him be *Lord.* Finally at the end of ourselves and our resources, we said, "We're done living in our own strength, Lord. Take over. Our lives are yours." Over the years that followed, as we started trusting Him and letting go of our way of doing things, He began to shape us and prepare us to walk down the path that ultimately led to Southeast Asia.

The gospel is life changing. The gospel is life-*saving.*

It definitely saved and changed my life. Before I met Christ, I was on the fast track to destruction. I grew up in an incredibly dysfunctional home with infidelity, divorce, drugs, alcoholism, abuse, and broken relationships. I was taught that education, position, and money were the keys to success and that religion was an obligation. Still, none of the people around me seemed very happy with any of those things.

When the gospel impacted my life, it transformed my heart and I became a new person. For the first time I felt valued and loved for who I was in Christ, not for anything I had done. God, in His grace, rescued me from an unhealthy family background and gave me a strong, healthy, and loving immediate family of my own. I finally learned the reason I was born, to glorify God by using the gifts He put in me to tell others about Christ.

I had no background or formal training to go where God led our family in 2006. I only knew that when God tells you to do something, you do it. And what gave us the courage and the confidence to follow Him every step of the way, even when it felt scary and difficult, was simply that we believed that *every one* of God's promises is true. Stepping out in obedience was a natural response to the overwhelming grace that had been poured into my life, knowing that we were being led by a completely trustworthy God.

But what happened between 2006 and 2009 isn't really what is important. It is what happened 2,000 years ago that matters. I can't receive the gospel, something I don't deserve, and not let others in on it too. In a world that is constantly seeking purpose, affirmation, healing, and hope in all the wrong places, it excites me to meet people whose hearts and lives have been impacted by the gospel.

But the gospel doesn't just excite me, it burdens me too. Jesus Christ died for every person living in every country in every part of the world. I can't be content to live a fat and happy life in America, knowing that millions of people in the world could die without ever hearing.

Dave Davidson said, "If you found a cure for cancer, wouldn't it be inconceivable to hide it from the rest of mankind? How much more inconceivable to keep silent the cure from the eternal wages of death."

Americans sometimes forget that there are many places in the world where the gospel is still unknown. Most Americans know what church is, and most Americans have heard the name of Jesus. I am fairly certain that not all of the people who have heard the name of

Jesus know who He really was or why He came to earth. But if they want to find out, there are opportunities in our country for them to hear. It isn't that way for those who live in other parts of the world, where the majority of the earth's population lives. And that compels me to go, because "How are they to call on him in whom they have not believed? And how are they to believe in him of whom they have never heard? And how are they to hear without someone preaching? And how are they to preach unless they are *sent*?" (Romans 10:14–15).

WHAT ARE *YOU* WAITING FOR?

In 1985, Curt and I were working in Manhattan. We both grew up near New York City, and we were in our first jobs out of college.

As we rode a bus home at night to our tiny New Jersey apartment, we would frequently muse over what we considered our five-year plan. We were just twenty-two and twenty-three years old when we got married, so we had a lot of goals we wanted to achieve. It seemed important to lay them all out and work out a schedule, of sorts, for our plans. That way we wouldn't lose sight of any of them.

But all these years later I can't remember what our five-year plan included. I still see young people who have a desire to plan out their lives. Truthfully though, can we even know where we will be in five years? I don't see anywhere in Scripture where God says he leads us in increments of five years. And when I read the Bible, I see just the opposite. God gets hold of a person's life and turns it upside-down overnight. Moses was herding sheep on the backside of nowhere when God told him to return to Egypt and confront the world's most powerful head of state. It's hard to imagine a more abrupt, or more extreme, turnaround in a person's life.

And while it's true that Moses had been following sheep around for forty years, getting from Midian to Egypt took far less than five years.

Here's another reason I have trouble with the five-year plan. I've had many conversations with people who say they have heard God's call—some for a short term, others for a long-term, and some to do something different while remaining right where they are. So I ask them: "What are you waiting for?"

I don't know if they are so committed to their plan that they overlooked the idea that when God calls, you answer now, not in five years. But their response to my question is "Now is not the right time."

If right now is not a good time then it's never going to be the right time. Once a Christian really believes that all of God's promises are true, then following through with obedience to God's call is not a hard decision. It is a simple matter of following a trustworthy God. This is normal discipleship and not a radical or special way to live.

Following Jesus as His disciple requires a number of things. Willingness, an open heart, the ability to hear his call, and the faith to follow him in obedience. A disciple is a follower, and following any leader involves obedience. One of my heroes on this side of eternity, Elisabeth Elliot, says about raising children that "anything short of first-time obedience is disobedience." That might sound harsh, but to me it's absolutely true. I feel the same rule applies to adults who say they want to obey God's call.

Unless you are in medical school and are waiting to graduate and complete your residency before you head overseas, I would ask: "What are you holding onto so tightly that you are afraid to let go of? What is so important to you that you are waiting before you respond to God's call?"

J. D. Greear has said, "Your life indicates what's important to you by what you are willing to give up."

It's the 'giving up' part that really scares some people. We feel more comfortable when we can put our trust in things that we can see, like 401ks and investment portfolios and a steady paycheck. But faith means trusting and believing in something that you can't see. I know from personal experience that trusting in yourself is a trap that will keep you from fully experiencing God's provision and faithfulness.

What looks like giving things up to the world is actually gain, and not just in this life but for eternity. Remember, you can't out-give God. But you'll never find out unless you try Him.

What are you waiting for?

*"He is no fool who gives what he cannot keep
to gain what he cannot lose."*

—Jim Elliot (October 8, 1927–January 8, 1956)